Thalatt:
Spirit of th(
ISBN 978-0-9563

GW00537869

By Peter and Rita I
who have asserted their rights under the
Copyright, Designs and Patents Act, 1988
to be identified as authors of this work.

Published by Phillips Design Publishing
Tollesbury
phillipsdesignpublishing.co.uk
© All photographs Copyright Phillips Design unless otherwise stated

Printed by Think Ink of Ipswich

Acknowledgements

The authors would like to thank Nick Hayward and Joe Brannigan of ECST, Andy Harman, Jerry Thompson Catharine Lockwood and Keith Webb for their contributions, and Charles Trail of SSBR for his proof reading.

Contents

Foreword

In writing this book we did not want to tell the story of the restoration of another old wooden sailing vessel, nor did we want to just tell the history of one.

Indeed, throughout this book we have tried to steer clear of the word "Restoration" with its implication of returning something to a former state, rather preferring "Refurbishment", being more in keeping with an intention to fit something for future use.

Thames sailing barges have evolved over the years and continue to do so. Though no longer used for carrying commercial cargo, the three dozen or so still active serve a useful purpose as charter vessels, private yachts and for corporate entertainment. *Thalatta* however is different!

Since the mid 1960's she has been a dedicated school ship, earning her keep with the East Coast Sail Trust, bringing the immense benefits of developing team work and self reliance to thousands of young people from all walks of life.

From the beginning, the project to refurbish and modernise *Thalatta* was intended to look forward and equip her to continue her present role for the next hundred years rather than merely to preserve a piece of history, however important. The standard of workmanship, materials and equipment incorporated in the project was always set against the test of "Will it last another hundred years?" Throughout this book we have tried to tell a story from the perspective of the people involved with *Thalatta* so we are very grateful to those kind souls whose adventures we have been privileged to include.

Where we have used contemporary articles written either by ourselves or others we have done little or nothing in the way of subsequent editing. What we lose in grammatical perfection, we feel is more than made up for by the immediacy and spontaneity of the text.

The photographs used in this book come mainly from our own collection, those which do not are either the property of the East Coast Sail Trust Ltd or Mr. Joe Brannigan, Chairman of ECST. In both cases we are extremely grateful for permission to use them.

Rita and Peter Phillips

Prologue

Thalatta is a Thames sailing barge, but what is a Thames sailing barge and why *Thalatta*?

Briefly, by Thames sailing barge we mean a flat bottomed cargo carrying vessel equipped with lee boards to help with directional stability rather than an external keel. Internally a wooden or more usually steel girder or "Keelson" provides rigidity as an internal backbone.

The shape and form of the Thames barges evolved over many years but in the context of this book we refer to that form we are familiar with today and which developed over the latter part of the Nineteenth and first half of the Twentieth Centuries.

Sail plans could be ketch rigged, with sails on both main and mizzen masts supported by horizontal booms, or spritsail rigged with sails supported by sprits rising from the masts at an angle. A combination of the two, sprit rigged mains'l and ketch rigged mizzen is inelegantly referred to as a "Mulie" (A cross breed)!

The mulie rig, with its tall mizzen provided a more even distribution of sail area between the two masts, thus allowing the main mast and sprit to be shorter and more manageable in open sea conditions. This made it the rig of choice for the bigger coasting barges.

These larger barges owe their origins in many ways as much to the schooners and brigantines which served the East Coast as to the nimble little spritsail barges serving the small creeks and estuaries and of course the "London river", the Thames.

In their heyday the Thames barges carried just about any cargo which could be carried from one place to another, very much fulfilling the function of today's lorries.

There were some two thousand or so sailing barges in use at the turn of the twentieth century, ranging from the likes of the little forty one foot long *Cygnet* plying her trade in the small farm creeks of Suffolk to the mighty ninety foot plus coasting barges such as *Cambria, Hydrogen* and of course, *Thalatta.*

One vital role of the Thames barge was supplying the bustling City of London with feed for its horse drawn transport system. Return trips would be made with the resulting straw and manure from the metropolis, known as "The London mixture", to be used as fertiliser for the East Coast farms. True recycling.

In addition to Thalatta both Cambria (left) and Hydrogen (right) remain active in 2012

Why name the barge *Thalatta?* Here we delve into Greek mythology where *Thalassa* personified the primeval spirit of the sea. Mating with her male counterpart *Pontos*, she gave birth to the tribes of fish. Although not generally given human form, *Thalassa* appears in the fables of Aesop as a woman formed of sea water rising out of the ocean.

Roman mosaics also depict her as a woman rising from the sea, with crab-claw like horns, clothed in seaweed and holding a ship's oar.

Now generally used to mean "The sea" *Thalassa* represents the word in the *Ionian* form of Greek, the classical version of the language, the one in which the early Christian Gospels would have been written.

In the earlier *Attic* or Athenian form of the language the word would be spelt *Thalatta*. *Attic* began to give way generally to *Ionian* following the writing reforms carried out in Athens in 403 BC.

How McLearon's came to name their barge *Thalatta* is another story. The most likely explanation is that the square rigged ship *Thalatta* of Liverpool had been laying in the Harwich harbour for some time and that this had inspired the naming.

Given the version of the spelling used this seems very likely though the use of classical references was common in the naming of barges at this time.

Shortly before completing this work we were lucky enough to receive an e-mail from Jerry Thompson offering an original document which he had rescued from a skip in Harwich when the old Harbour Board had been cleaned out!

The document in question was a statement of claim and pleadings In the High Court of Justice, Probate, Divorce and admiralty Division (Admiralty). with Writs issued on the 28 March, 1905.

Between the owners, master and crew of the steam tug "Nubia" (Plaintiffs)
And
The owners of the ship "Thalatta" her cargo and freight   (Defendants)
And
Between the owners, master and crew of the steam tug "Challenge" (Plaintiffs)
And
The owners of the ship or vessel "Thalatta" her cargo and freight (Defendants)

The document tells in graphic detail the events leading to the sailing ship *Thalatta* being held at Harwich and thus possibly serving as the inspiration for the naming of McLearon's barge. We quote here excerpts which we hope will give a flavour of the events. The story is initially set out by the *Thalatta's* owners:

Shortly before 6 a.m. on March 25 the "Thalatta" a full rigged ship built of iron of 1.748 tons net register was in the English Channel off St. Catharine's in the course of a voyage from San Francisco to Ipswich with a cargo of barley. The "Thalatta" had encountered heavy weather during her voyage which left her with a list to starboard.
In the circumstances the master of the "Thalatta" contracted with the master of the tug "Gauntlet" for the sum of £55 to tow the "Thalatta" to the buoys in Butterman's Bay or if there was water to the docks in Ipswich. (Defence)

All did not go smoothly however as the *Gauntlet* had apparently sustained some damage to her propeller which prevented her towing *Thalatta* into Harwich harbour against the wind and tide. Consequently the tug *Challenge*, with the same owners, was engaged to take her place.

At about 3 a.m. on March 27 *Challenge* proceeded to tow *Thalatta* under the direction of the Pilot on board *Thalatta*. The vessels were nearing the Cliff Foot Buoy when;

The "Thalatta" which had a list to starboard and had been sluggish on her helm failed to answer her helm and to follow the "Chal-

lenge" and the latter's helm had to be hard -a –ported she had to tow broad off the "Thalatta's" starboard bow to get her to answer her helm. After a time the "Thalatta" began to come to and immediately she did so being apparently by the tide she took a sudden run to starboard and in spite of the efforts of the tug which at considerable risk as quickly as possible crossed her bow to prevent her she ran aground between the Gas and the Cliff Buoys and remained fast. (Plaintiffs – Challenge)

Whilst some of the steering references may seem strange to us, at the time, it was usual for steering orders on ships to be given as "Tiller orders", relating to which side of the vessel the tiller was to be moved. Since the tiller is forward of the rudder's pivot point, the tiller's movement is reversed at the rudder, giving the impression that orders were given "the wrong way round". For example, to turn a ship to port the helmsman would be given the order "starboard helm". The tiller arm would then be moved across to the starboard side of the ship thus giving port rudder.

When the ships wheel was introduced this was simply turned in the desired direction (turn the wheel to port and the ship will go to port). Tiller Orders remained however and although many maritime nations had abandoned the convention by the end of the 19th century, Britain retained it until 1933.

There are two sides to every story they say and the owners of *Thalatta* had a different version of events;

At about 5.30 a.m. the tide having been changed to ebb the "Thalatta" in tow of the "Challenge" rounded Beach Head Buoy under a port helm. The "Thalatta" when she had rounded the buoy was headed towards the Cliff Foot Buoy but the "Challenge" negligently and improperly and without receiving any orders from the "Thalatta" got broad on to the starboard bow of the "Thalatta" giving her a sheer to starboard against a starboard helm. The pilot of the "Thalatta" waved to the "Challenge" to go back to the port bow which she subsequently did but she was not sufficiently powerful to prevent the "Thalatta" which had been canted partly athwart the tide from taking ground on the bank to the north of Beach End Buoy.(Defence)

Further light on events is shed by the report from *Nubia*, a steam tug of 102 tons gross registered and six crew. She also had a claim for salvage based on her part in the re-floating of *Thalatta*.

At about 6 a.m. on March 27 1905 the "Nubia" was in Harwich Harbour in attendance on the dredger working in that harbour when the "Thalatta" in tow of a tug was seen coming in. The weather was thick with rain the wind fresh and squally from the south-westward and the tide about two hours ebb running strong. As the vessels rounded the Beach End the ship was seen to drive aground on the shoal to the eastward of the Cliff Foot Buoy. The "Nubia" at once went to her help and found the vessel fast aground heading to the N.E. and her tug unable to move her. The tug master hailed the ship and was at once engaged to get the vessel afloat. (Plaintiff – Nubia)

Initial attempts to re-float the ship met with no success. However with the coming of the flood tide, the tugs were able to free *Thalatta* and she eventually was taken safely into Harwich Port. Once more there is a difference of opinion as to the extent of the peril;

By the prompt and skilful services of the tug "Thalatta" and her valuable cargo were saved from a position of grave peril. The ship was hard and fast the tides were taking off and without the help of a powerful tug the ship must have broken her back or greatly strained and injured herself and her cargo. (Plaintiffs-Nubia)

The said services were of a perfectly simple and easy description and were attended by no circumstances involving difficulty or danger to the tugs or either of them. The sea throughout the day was smooth and the wind during the day fell from moderate breeze to dead calm. The "Thalatta" was never in any danger of loss or injury of herself or her cargo being grounded upon a bank of sand and shingle in 14 ft of water at low water. (Defence)

There were further claims and counter claims as to fault and degree of assistance and indeed to the value of the ship and cargo. The owners at least were in no doubt as to what they considered the value of their ship, cargo and freight.

An *Affidavit of Values* was sworn before a Commissioner for Oaths by James A Milroy for the owners on 2 May 1905 which stated;

The "Thalatta" is a full rigged ship belonging to the port of Liverpool of 1,793 tons gross and 1,748 tons net. She is 263 ft. in length and 39 ft. 1 in beam.

The "Thalatta "at the time in question was on a voyage from San Francisco to Ipswich laden with a cargo consisting of 2,754 tons of barley.

In the course of the said voyage the "Thalatta" experienced very heavy weather and sustained considerable damage and her value at the time of the alleged salvage services was £4000 and no more.

I have caused enquiries to be made and am informed and believe that the total value of the said cargo exclusive of freight was £14,901 7s 6d and no more.

The gross freight payable on delivery of the said cargo at Ipswich amounted to £3,098 but in order to earn the said freight the following expenses had to be incurred viz. cost of discharging and port charges £336 which amount deducted from the gross freight leaves £2,762 as the net freight at risk at the time of the said salvage services.

At the time of writing we have been unable to discover the outcome of the case which, whilst not of great importance to our story, would make an interesting conclusion to the tale.

Photo from State Library of South Australia ref PRG 1373/9/37

The sailing ship Thalatta at Port Adelaide circa 1905

Chapter One
Birth of a Thames Sailing Barge

The Thames sailing barge *Thalatta* was built at W B McLearon's shipyard in Harwich over the winter of 1905-6, one of a pair of barges said to have been built on speculation of finding a buyer.

The other barge was *Ena* destined for delivery to R W Paul's the Maltsters. She enjoyed a long and distinguished life including featuring in the TV programme "Salvage Squad" a few years ago. Sadly, at the time of writing, *Ena* is in a sorry state at Hoo in Kent, where she remains despite having been put up for sale at the end of 2010.

Clues to *Thalatta's* beginnings can be found in contemporary reports, the first of which is in the form of a document held by ECST and which appears to have been typed in the late 1970's. This clearly quotes from a local account of the construction of the two barges;

"In 1905-6 the Mayor of Harwich is William Mclearon.
He runs a coal business, and builds wooden vessels in the former Naval Shipyard there.

His contracts to build wooden lightships for the Corporation of Trinity house have taught him a great deal about constructing a really strong vessel. He has been studying the qualities of the local trading ketches and fishing smacks, and comparing them with the spritsail rigged Thames Estuary barges which are commonplace in the busy harbour.

Now, as a speculation, he is building an unusual coasting barge, incorporating some of these ideas. As she takes shape, she arouses local interest. Onlookers comment that her fine head belongs more to a fishing smack than to a barge. Her cargo-carrying capacity is less than other barges of a similar size being built elsewhere on the coast, the HYDRO-GEN and the CAMBRIA, nor is she designed primarily for speed like the EDITH MAY now under construction by Mr. Cann on the other Harwich barge yard.

But the hull promises to steer well, and to be particularly capable and comfortable at sea. She is narrow on the bottom, with long runs aft to a neat stern frame."

The comment that *Thalatta* (72 reg.ton) would have a lesser cargo carrying capacity than *Hydrogen* (98 reg.ton) or *Cambria* (79 reg.ton) being "barges of a similar size" is a little disingenuous as both are wider in the beam and both are longer,though *Cambria* only very slightly.

"As the hull nears completion, McLearon leaves it un tarred so that

the purple stain may bleed out of the oak, and the showers of rain soon make the timber as dark as though it had indeed been tarred. As yet she has no owner, and no name".

The piece continues, now clearly written from a 1970's perspective;

Perhaps it is McLearon himself who gives her the name of the fine sailing ship which has been lying in the Harbour for some time. The handsome lines of the full-rigged ship THALATTA of Liverpool would have undoubtedly taken his eye.

And further, clearly relating to a later time;

A Mistley bargeman remarks admiringly as he looks down on her decks from aloft, years later "she sits on the water like a little old seagull this one."

Built on speculation or not, *Thalatta* was already owned by Fredrick Horlock when she was first registered at 10 am on 14 February 1906 having been purchased for £200 with a Mortgage from Barclays Bank at a rate of 5 per cent.

To put this into perspective, it is likely that the weekly rate of pay for a shipwright at this time would have been less than 30 shillings. This figure is referred to as the pre 1914 rate by the Board of Arbitration set up under the Wages (temporary regulation) Acts 1918/19 in settling a dispute, *W.B. Mclearon v Shipbuilders and Constructors association (1919).* Not much, but considerably better than the agricultural labourer's 15 shillings per week of the same period!

The launch of a new barge was a sufficiently momentous event to make the local press with *The Evening Star & Daily Herald for Ipswich* carrying the following report.

"An interesting ceremony was witnessed in the shipbuilding yard of Mr, W McLearon, at Harwich today (Tuesday 6 February 1906) when a new barge, which has been built in the yard, was launched in the presence of a large number of people. The barge, which was christened the Thalatta, is owned by Mr, Fredrick William Horlock, the well known boat owner of Mistley. She is a fine business like looking craft, being 89 feet long, beam 20 feet 6 inches, depth 7 feet 6 inches, and her tonnage is 160. She will be used for the coasting and continental trade.

The barge was decorated with flags and the christening ceremony was performed by Mr. Horlock's little daughter, Coralie Clare, who broke a bottle of Champagne over the bows, after which the vessel glided beautifully into the water, amid three hearty cheers, the launch being a highly successful one. The Thalatta immediately proceeded to Mistley to load a cargo of wheat for London, and will afterwards proceed to the Continent." (NB the tonnage referred to is not her Registered tonnage)

Received wisdom for many years was that *Thalatta* was rigged from the beginning as a ketch and did not change to a spritsail rig until later in life. Certainly we know for sure that she was ketch rigged in 1916 (when she was listed as 72 ton as opposed to 67 in later lists) and spritsail rigged by 1934 because she appears as such in the Merchant Navy Lists for those years.

John Kemp (and he should know-see later!) in his *"A fair wind for London"* relates that Fred Horlock, having made up his mind to buy one of the two barges being built by McLearon, insisted "Against all advice" to have her as a spritsail barge rather than with a boom and gaff ketch rig which was more usual for the large coasting barges working away from sheltered waters.

The same source tells us that *Thalatta's* first trip was made under the captaincy of James Alliston of Mistley whose initial voyage was to London to pick up a cargo for Lowestoft. Having arrived on 26 February, we are told that *Thalatta* next set out for Hull before returning to Mistley.

On 24 March *Thalatta* set out for Ipswich where a cargo of beans was loaded for Nieupoort on the river Yasr in Flanders. From thence a cargo was loaded for Antwerp before the return journey was made.

Whether it was the trials and tribulations of taking a spritsail rig across the North Sea on this occasion or at a later date is not recorded but it was not long before *Thalatta* was fitted with a gaff and boom mains'l, thus avoiding the dangers recorded by John Kemp later;

"Rollin' about off the in the middle o' the North Sea with a sixty foot spreet aloft in a gale o' wind" had frightened her skipper (James Alliston) more than once and that *"He was a man as took some frightening".*(A conversation with one Freddy Bloyce, reported in *"A fair wind for London"*).

Full advantage was to be taken of the new rig in the years which led up to the start of the first World War in 1914. In this period *Thalatta* made numerous journeys from Mistley and Ipswich, often loaded with malt. She went North to Newcastle and Sunderland, West to Appledore, the delightful little village on the River Torridge near Bideford in North Devon, across to Ireland to visit Dublin, Wexford and Wicklow and across the Channel to continental ports.

Not all *Thalatta's* voyages were routine smooth sailing by any means and she suffered two narrow escapes both of which could have proved fatal but for the skill of her skipper, still Captain Alliston.

On Thursday 10 December 1908 she was on the way from Sunderland to London fully loaded when, despite a fair forecast, benign winds and a gentle sea rapidly erupted into a severe storm. *Thalatta,* having fought the weather for three days was eventually towed into Lowestoft with a broken main gaff and a split mains'l.

So bad was the storm that the barges *Ernest Piper, Gannet, Leslie West, Prima Donna, Joseph* and *William and Mary* were either lost or severely damaged. Other vessels were also to suffer including a lugger from Yarmouth which sadly lost three men drowned.

On 15 January 1909 *Thalatta* was making her way down the River Thames at Blackwell Reach, when she was struck amidships by the steamer *Forth*, doing considerable damage. After temporary repairs at Shrubsall's yard *Thalatta* was eventually able to continue her journey and safely deliver her cargo of maize.

The "Great War" of 1914 brought a change of work for *Thalatta* and her Master for throughout 1915 they were occupied with the dull but vital work of lightering in the Thames. 1916 was a more adventurous year however as *Thalatta* found herself once more voyaging across to the continent. Mines and U boats now added to the usual maritime hazards as she made voyages from Shoreham on the Sussex coast to Dieppe with pig iron for the war effort. Pity the poor crew member stationed in the bow looking out for mines on such trips!

Thalatta was sold to the Wynnfield Shipping Company of Grimsby on 22 May 1917. One of the first things her new owners did was to fit a 70 h.p. two cycle vertical oil engine built by Plenty & Sons of Newbury. This engine was installed in what had been the skipper's cabin aft.

The crew, now including an engineer for the first time, had the converted forward hold. *Thalatta's* registration as a sailing vessel was cancelled and she was re registered as an "Auxiliary Ketch".

Referring to the writings of John Kemp once more, we read that Percy Richmond, having held the post of mate for some time, was now elevated to the position of skipper.

The period until the Armistice in 1918 was spent mainly as a supply vessel for the Humber boom defences. These defences, comprising the Haile Sand Fort and the Bull Sand Fort were started in 1915 to offer protection from invasion and the incursion of German U Boats. The fortifications were armed with 6 inch guns and up to 200 men to defend against the former and a large net to catch the latter. Unglamorous as this work was, it was, none the less, essential.

The end of hostilities did not mean the end of war related work for *Thalatta*. Now under the command of Herbert Body from Southend, she spent the period from 1919 to 1921 regularly making trips to the Continent with materials for the post war rebuilding of Europe's shattered infrastructure.

One of *Thalatta's* regular runs at this time would have been into Flanders, scene of three battles of Ypres and inspiration for the poem "*In Flanders fields*" by John McCrae, which in turn gave rise to the now familiar icon of remembrance "The Flanders poppy". *Thalatta* also found herself making journeys to Paris, Antwerp, Brussels and Rotterdam.

Although as related, Herbert Body had *Thalatta* at this time he does not seem to have been her only skipper. It is said that Fred Grant, who apparently first went to sea at the age of sixteen, regularly took the barge on the Shoreham to Dieppe run. Charles Munn is also recorded as having command on at least one trip from Grimsby to Paris.

Less war ravaged destinations were to follow with trips to Torquay carrying cement, to Greenhithe with china clay brought from Fowey in Cornwall and even a cargo of granite chippings from the Channel Islands all being noted.

In May 1923 Herbert Body purchased *Thalatta* from Wynnfield's and took the significant step of removing her engine and, while keeping her gaff rigged mizzen, replacing her boom rigged mainsail with a spritsail thus turning *Thalatta* into a mulie.

The reason for this change is not recorded but there may be a clue in John Kemp's writing when he relates how;

"If two men and a lad had been a sufficient complement in the days of sail, a different situation now existed, and the fore hold was decked over and converted to accommodate a further four hands, one of them the "motor-engineer" who looked after the new machinery."

It is likely that any new owner would be looking for the most economical rig possible, and two crew are cheaper than six!

Ownership may have changed but *Thalatta's* working life did not to any great extent as she continued to trade between the ports on the North East and Southern coasts of England including, it is believed, at least one trip to Lewes in Sussex to deliver materials for work on the railway line. Thalatta also continued her regular trips across the channel to the continent.

On 5 August 1933 *Thalatta* changed hands once more when she was purchased by R and W Paul Ltd (Maltsters) of Ipswich for the sum of £450.

We know that *Thalatta* remained a spritsail sailing barge from her entries in the Merchant Navy lists of the period which record
Her as;

R W Paul 67 ton Spritsail (Formerly a motor vessel)- MNL 1934
And

RW Paul 67 ton Spritsail   *MNL 1938*

Photo courtesy ECST

Thalatta pictured as a motor auxiliary, probably in 1920

Thalatta's work at this time was largely taking imported grain from the Royal Docks in London to Ipswich with return journeys made with malt, flour or animal feed, this was standard fare for a Paul's barge and work she would do for many years.

Legendry barge skipper Bob Ruffles had charge in 1934 and remained so throughout the war years. Of other crew members, we know that Mo King was mate during the mid war years and that a very young Ivan Hazleton signed on as third hand at a wage of £1 18s 0d (£1.90) (*Time before the mast* - Chaffcutter books)

Despite the dangers of this time the one incident where we are aware of his barge getting into trouble was the year after the war ended!

In 1946 while near the Gunfleet Sands, where the elegant wind farm now resides, *Thalatta* got into sufficient difficulties to require the help of the Clacton lifeboat, the *Edward Z Drezden* which towed her into Brightlingsea.

This lifeboat, named after the London merchant who had the "English Dresden" 78.53 carat white diamond cut from a Brazilian stone in the mid Nineteenth century, enjoyed a long and illustrious career serving the Clacton area from 1929 to 1952 before moving on The Orkneys.

In 1947 *Thalatta* had a new skipper when Joe Lucas took over. Joe a Manningtree man, remained master until replaced by Charlie Webb at the start of the 1950's. Joe was to feature in one of *Thalatta's* rare television appearances when, in 1973, he recalled his time on board *Thalatta* for a TV documentary.

In the interview Joe recalls that as a young man in 1943 he joined the barge at Lowestoft for his first trip. They set out for London to collect 700 cwt of maize which they transported to Norwich. Joe recalled another frequent cargo was "Cow cake"- a concentrated feed for cattle in the form of cubes or blocks.

Joe also related that it was common to take wheat up to Greens flour mills at Brantham. This journey however involved negotiating passage under the hump backed bridge at Catawade. This could be achieved by anchoring with the nose of the barge as far under the bridge as possible then waiting for the tide to come in. With *Thalatta* just floating there was about three inches of clearance under the bridge, just sufficient to edge carefully through. Once clear the skipper was free to make the rest of the journey at his leisure!

Film of *Thalatta* shown with the interview revealed a barge externally very similar to her current form except for the wheel house carried at that time.

Chapter Two
Out of Trade

This is not the place to attempt a full history of the Thames sailing barge or it's gradual demise as a cargo carrying vessel. However a brief look may help to put *Thalatta's* story into perspective.

The heyday of the Thames sailing barge is usually reckoned to have been towards the end of the Nineteenth and beginning of the Twentieth Centuries. By this time it's shape had evolved from a shovel-ended, lighter-like form to the straight prow and transom stern vessels we are now familiar with. Sail plans were either ketch or, more usually sprit rigs and there was an abundance of trade to be had.

The coming of the internal combustion engine and the expansion of the rail network gradually had their effect however. At first the drop in trade was far from dramatic, however it was measurable.

The excellent *"Barge Trust"* web site quotes a figure of over 2,000 Thames barges being registered in 1907. If we peruse the Merchant Navy List entries for barges on the *"Mersea Island Museum"* site we find that this figure had dropped to approximately 1,850 by 1916.

This period saw other changes to the barges as they strove to compete. Wood is bulky and heavy material for building so many of the diminishing number of barges built in the early twentieth century were constructed from metal. This gave a greater available hold space for a given hull size compared to a wooden barge as internal bracing and bulky frames were not required. Lighter build weight meant that they could be faster as well.

More and more barges acquired diesel engines, either to augment sail power or to replace it. Whatever the innovations, the Thames barge started to lose ground. By 1934 the MNL lists less than 750 barges, less than half the number of eighteen years earlier.

A reduction in trade for the barges inevitably and logically meant a reduction in new buildings, thus not only was natural wastage not replaced but the ravages of the war years were not made up.

World War Two saw the barges performing heroically around our coast, whether as lighters, cargo carriers (those without engines were reckoned to be safer for carrying ammunition for instance) or as bases for the barrage balloons as part of our aerial defences against dive bombers.

Thames barges and their crews participated in the evacuation of British and allied troops at the fall of France, often under heavy fire.

It is believed that approximately thirty sailing and auxiliary Thames barges took part in "Operation Dynamo" from 28 May 1940 to 4 June. In this time they played their part in bringing back about three hundred and forty thousand allied servicemen.

The rescue of the British Expeditionary Force from the beaches of Dunkirk was not achieved without a heavy price being paid.

In an attempt to protect the rescuing fleet the RAF sent sweeps deep into France to intercept enemy aircraft before they reached the beach head. The heavily outnumbered fighters, now included for the first time the nimble Spitfires which had been kept back for home defence. With the sturdy Hurricanes they flew nearly five thousand sorties over the period and suffered 100 losses. The Luftwaffe suffered more and had, if only briefly, had to concede air superiority for the first time in the war.

Despite the best efforts of the RAF, those enemy aircraft which did get through strafed and bombed repeatedly and casualties were heavy.

Of those Thames barge losses we can trace, we know that R and W Paul alone lost three, *Aide, Barbara Jean* and *Doris*. F T Everard are known to have lost *Ethel Everard* while Wakely Bros lost *Duchess*.

As with other classes of vessel, many of the barges did return however and some are still active today. *Pudge* owned and operated by the Thames Sailing Barge Trust brought back at least three hundred troops as well as survivors of a tug and two barges sunk by bombing.

Besides *Pudge*, three other barges are currently sailing which The Association of Dunkirk Little Ships list as members. These are *Cabby*, which operates as a charter barge. *Dawn*, based at West Mersea and which featured in the brilliant Griff Rhys Jones "Lost Highways" programme and *Greta* operated by Steve Norris at Whitstable.

A few other veterans such as *Tollesbury*, which also survived the London IRA bombings survive and are subjects of restoration projects while others like *Ena* are, at best, hanging on to existence by a thread!

As related *Thalatta* did not go to Dunkirk nor was her wartime employment particularly glamorous. The carriage of grain and foodstuffs around our coasts was however an important part of our wartime survival and one which Hitler did his best to prevent as *Bankside*, *Emma* and *Gertrude May* at least found to their cost.

With the end of the war came a Britain much changed from that of 1938 and, as with so many returning heroes, many of the barges found work hard to come by.

In 1948 *Thalatta* went to Richard's shipyard in Lowestoft where an 80 hp Ruston and Hornsby marine diesel was fitted. She did, however, retain at least a mains'l and tops'l as can be seen in the picture below.

Photo courtesy ECST

Thalatta pictured in 1956, still retaining much of her sailing gear.

Thalatta's appearance was to change in 1958, when Ivan Hazleton joined her as mate to Bob Wells with Stanley Missen as third hand. Ivan relates in his *"Time before the mast"*, how the "Worn out gear and lee boards" were removed and she "Relied on her engine alone".

In many ways the fate of the Thames barge was settled by the revolution in the way goods were moved round the UK in the second half of the twentieth century.

Horse drawn and steam road transport was already in serious decline by the start of the Second World War, being replaced by the motor lorry. Although the conflict prolonged their usefulness, the end of petrol rationing in 1950 sounded their death knell for general use.

Government statistics for the period tell us that the number of motor lorries registered for road use grew by 50% between 1946 and 1952, although size, weight and speed restrictions had not changed since the 1930's. These were to be liberalised however in Acts passed in 1956 and 1964.

A paper to the Royal Statistical Society presented by K F Glover and D N Miller in 1954, *"The outlines of the goods transport industry"* quoted the following figures:

Road Transport	72%	of goods carried (in tons)
Rail	24%	
Coastal shipping	3%	
Canal	1%	

These figures were based on a sample taken in September 1952.

Thalatta was doing her share of the 3% at this time as can be seen from some of her log entries:

Sailed 26.10.51 London to Ipswich 610 qrts Wheat from SS Warkworth
Arrived 27.10.51
The return journey to London was made empty.
Then
Sailed 3.11.51 London to Felixstowe 655 qrts Wheat from SS Daleby
Arrived 4.11.51
Sailed 13.11.51 London to Ipswich 638 qrts Barley from
SS Muristan Arrived 14.11.51

An increase in the numbers, speed and payload of lorries, would mean nothing without the roads on which they travel of course.

A paper by M V Lowson, entitled *"Surface transport history in UK"* tells us that in the decade before 1950, 5175 miles of trunk roads were constructed, the highest ten year figure for any form of surface transport system recorded. The next nearest figure being the 4321 miles of railway constructed in 1870. This expansion was to continue, albeit at a reduced rate over the following years.

With the expansion of the road network and the desire for speed, coastal shipping was bound to suffer. Later, containerisation and the demise of many of the smaller ports all played their part.

For the sail powered barge the writing had been on the wall for some time. With the reduction of trade for coastal shipping the old barges gradually found themselves out of work. Age took an increasing toll on their numbers as they became uneconomical to maintain and repair.

Thalatta was no different to her sisters, though she lasted longer than many. Inevitably, however time ran out for her as a cargo carrying barge.

Thalatta's last full year in trade was 1965, though some freights were taken in 1966. In that last full year she is recorded as having been at sea for a total of ninety seven days, carrying cargoes from London to Colchester, Faversham, Ipswich, Mistley and Rochford.

The ship's log for 1966 shows only two trips in January, one to London with malt and the other back to Ipswich with oilcake.

The next entry in the log, in a different hand, is for 13 October stating that she has 100 tons of wheat at Ipswich, lightering.The final entry for 1966 and first for 1967 are then recorded as:

      30/10/66   *Ipswich*   *Light* *1/11/66* *Maldon*
                             Refitting

   24/4/67   *Maldon*   *12 passengers* *28/4/67 Maldon*

13/10/66	Ipswich	100 Tons wheat lightering		
30/10/66	Ipswich	Light	1/11/66	Maldon
		Refitting		
24/4/67	Maldon	12 Passengers	28/4/67	Maldon
1/5/67	Maldon	12 Passengers	5/5/67	Colchester
5/5/67	Colchester	Light	6/5/67	Maldon
4/5/67	Maldon	12 Passengers	12/5/67	Maldon
15/5/67	Maldon	12 Passengers	19/5/67	Maldon
22/5/67	Maldon	12 Passengers	26/5/67	Maldon
29/5/67	Maldon	12 Passengers	2/6/67	Maldon
5/6/67	Maldon	12 Passengers	9/6/67	Maldon
12/6/67	Maldon	12 Passengers	16/6/67	Maldon
26/6/67	Maldon	12 Passengers	30/6/67	Maldon
1/7/67	Race day			
3/7/67	Maldon	12 Passengers	7/7/67	Maldon
10/7/67	Maldon	12 Passengers	14/7/67	Maldon
17/7/67	Maldon	12 Passengers	21/7/67	Maldon
24/7/67	Maldon	12 Passengers	28/7/67	~~Ipswich~~
31/7/67	Maldon	S' Apprentice	4/8/67	Ipswich
5/8/67	Ipswich	Ship yard		
9/8/67	Ipswich	5 Apprentices	10/8/67	Maldon
16/8/67	Maldon	6 Guests	18/8/67	Colchester

By late 1966 John Kemp's plans for using *Thalatta* for sail training were well laid as, to quote from *"A fair wind from London"* once more ;

"Apparently Roy Orvis had succeeded in persuading his superiors at R & W Paul of the worthiness of my project. I was able, with a little help from Hervey Benham to meet the remarkable generous terms they proposed. I became the owner of Thalatta in November 1966".

It is said that the purchase price was £1500. John goes on to recount two further tasks *Thalatta* undertook for Paul's before he fully took possession. One was a cargo of malt, for which he received the owners share of the freight!

"The other, more melancholy, was to scatter the ashes of her last professional skipper, Fred Roberts, on the River Orwell."

Neither of these last two trips seem to appear in the copy of the ships log reproduced here.

John's "project" was to see *Thalatta* through nearly fifty years of unbroken service as an educational vehicle before her refit brought a temporary halt to sailing at the end of the 2005 season.

Photo courtesy ECST

Thalatta pictured in 1964, looking much as she would when taken over by John Kemp.

Chapter Three
John Kemp-Master Mariner

The names of John Kemp and of *Thalatta* become unbreakably linked at this point and it would perhaps be as well to record a few notes on the life of the man who was to do so much to give the barge a new and useful lease of life. John Kemp was born in London in 1926 the son of Arthur (once "Larry Lynx"- racing correspondent of the People newspaper) and of Lucy.

Too young for regular war service John Kemp served in the Home Guard before being called up into the Bedfordshire and Hertfordshire Regiment (later absorbed into the Royal Anglia Regiment) in 1944.

Leaving the Army in 1946, his father having died just after the War, John and his mother spent many of the immediate post war years in the West Country and in Essex.

During his time in the West Country the young John developed a taste for writing, producing a number of articles on politics. In later life he was to go on to make contributions to the Essex press on such subjects as coastal life, short stories, amateur dramatics and even obituaries.

In 1957, John became a family man when he married Monica. The couple subsequently brought up three sons and a daughter.

Before undertaking his work with sail training, John was involved with the building of the power station at Bradwell as well as being employed at various times by Shell Oil and E. H. Bentall and Co, the agricultural machinery manufacturers.

A career working on the East Coast provided the basis for John's first book *"A fair wind for London"* which recalled his time at sea working on the Thames barges and which has supplied so much information for this publication. This first work was followed by two others, *"God's hungry sheep"*, a religious novel, and a collection of short stories set on the Essex coast called *"At the wash of oysters"*.

John was heavily involved in the early movement to preserve the Thames sailing barges, particularly in an active cargo carrying role. One of the first such ventures being the Thames Sailing Barge Trust. In 1952 an Exploratory Committee was formed by a small group of enthusiasts who realized that working sailing craft were disappearing from the British way of life and decided to do something about it. Plans were made to raise sufficient funds from public subscriptions to purchase a barge to be maintained perpetually in working condition under sail alone.

The trust acquired the sailing barge *Memory* in 1956, in the same year changing it's name to the Sailing Barge Preservation Society to avoid confusion with other organisations.

Inevitably perhaps, by 1959 trading had become difficult not only through a lack of cargoes but also because the *Memory* sustained damage when run down in fog, incurring expensive repairs.

In 1960 the Society wound up its affairs and its assets were given to the Foudroyant Trust, dedicated to sail training and latterly to the restoration of *HMS Trincomalee*. This classic Frigate, the oldest British warship afloat, has now been fully restored at Hartlepool.

John Kemp, without whom there would be no story
(Photo via wikimedia commons)

Chapter Four
Sail Training

With the demise of the Sailing Barge Preservation Society and at the suggestion of Hervey Benham, the proprietor of Essex County Newspapers, "Sailtrust Ltd" was formed as a partnership between John Kemp and Brian Beer, to use a Thames barge to work with young people.

Born in 1910, Hervey Benham was the prolific author of many books on the subject of Essex and the East Coast. Though *"Down Topsl'l"* is probably his best known, we particularly like his *"Sailing craft of East Anglia"* written with Roger Finch and giving perhaps the definitive account of the types of vessel to be found in those waters.

Hervey was editor of the *Essex County Standard* from 1943 to 1945, and with fellow newspaper proprietor Arnold Quick, helped pioneer the use of web offset lithography in the newspaper industry when adopting it for printing that newspaper in 1964.

An accomplished musician as well as writer, Hervey will be known to many as a great benefactor. In addition to his work setting up what was to become the East Coast Sail Trust, he founded the *Hervey Benham Charitable Trust* in 1978, which has the aim of helping talented individuals and groups and of keeping the North East Essex industrial and maritime heritage alive. It was Hervey who in an article describing a voyage on board *Thalatta*, coined the phrase "Five days in another world" which remains the motto of East Coast Sail Trust Ltd to this day.

John Kemp continued to skipper *Memory* which had now been converted from a cargo carrier to a sail training ship. Thus began a long association with young people and sail training, which was only to end with John's tragic early death in September 1987 having reached the comparatively tender age of sixty one.

Originally offering "adventure training" it was soon found that this alone did not pay so *Memory* was operated at weekends as a charter barge, said to be the first of her kind to undertake such work on a regular basis.

In April 1965 "Sailtrust". secured a contract with the London Borough of Redbridge to take parties of school children sailing for week long trips. These trips were to be run from April to October. This was good news for "Sailtrust", but it was to be less so for *Memory* as the regulations governing the use of charter vessels had recently been tightened by the Board of Trade and it proved to be impractical to modify the old barge to comply with the new requirements.

Although *Memory* was to pass out of school ship use, her days of working with young people were far from over as she was acquired by "Fellowship Afloat" (now FACT), a Christian charity for young people.

Acting as a base on the Tollesbury Saltings, *Memory* could accommodate up to 22 people who were thus able to enjoy the quiet rural surroundings of the Essex marshes, though when the wind whistles in from the East or the gulls are in full cry, quiet may not be exactly the word!

By 1990 *Memory's* chemical toilets and paraffin lighting had become outdated and the lightship *Trinity* had been purchased as a replacement.

Before *Trinity* could be made fully operational, a disastrous fire left *Memory* as nothing more than a hulk derelict on the marshes, though thankfully no one was injured. *Memory* remains in the same state today.

In November 1966 ownership of *Thalatta* passed from R.W.Paul's to John Kemp and thus she became a replacement for *Memory,* with John as skipper and with Hervy's daughter, Jane, as mate.

Jane Benham MBE, was a prolific and respected artist in her own right and a supporter of many charities. Sadly cut down by cancer in 1992 at the age of 49, Jane is commemorated by an annual Memorial Lecture.

Before *Thalatta* could be used in her new roll, work was required which again changed her appearance. As previously related her latter days as a cargo carrying barge had been spent under motor power. John Kemp now set about having her returned to sail with a spritsail main sail and with a ketch rigged mizzen, making her a mulie once more.

The formation of the East Coast Sail Trust in 1971 was to mark the turning point in the career not only of the sailing barge *Thalatta* but also in the lives of so many people who were able to enjoy and learn from the experience of the "Five days in another world" provided by the Trust.

John Kemp was to continue as skipper of *Thalatta* until his untimely death at her wheel in the mouth of the River Blackwater at "Bench Head" in 1987. (Ironically in the same year Hervey Benham passed away). This sad event required not a little subterfuge to keep the news from the young crew on board at the time.

The period in *Thalatta's* life when she was under the command of John Kemp with Jane Benham as mate is acknowledged to this day in the naming of the ships boats, one is *John* the other *Jane*!

Barges under the ECST flag were, and still are, known as "School ships" rather than as sail training vessels. This reflects the original concept of providing a floating classroom from which young people could discover at first hand the ecology, geography and maritime history of the area around the Thames Estuary, from Kent to Suffolk.

For a while the ECST operated another barge in tandem with *Thalatta*. This was the *Sir Alan Herbert* which was bought with the proceeds of an appeal made in the memory of the novelist, playwright and one-time MP, A P Herbert.

Although the programme was not originally designed to be specifically "Character building" in reality it was to prove to be very much so. The experience of having to work together and live together for five days was to mould very many disparate young crews into teams by the end of their stay on board.

Perhaps this would be a good time to introduce a little of the life and work on board *Thalatta* as a school ship.

View from Thalatta's wheel in 2005

Chapter Five
"Five days in another world"

The following is gleaned from the website of the former Nightingale High School (now long gone) and relates to a trip undertaken in 1974. The following is given as the daily schedule for that trip:

0700 hrs *Duty team up and preparing breakfast*
0715 *Deck team up and scrubbing round the deck*
0730 *Duty team to breakfast*
0800 *Watches change and retiring deck team to breakfast*
1030 *Inspection of quarters and galley*
1100 *Mid morning snack*
1230 *Lunch-duty team*
1300 *Watches change and retiring deck team to lunch*
1530 *Inspection of quarters and galley*
1730 *Tea-duty team*
1800 *Watches change and retiring deck team to tea*
2200 *Lights out*

"The week on the Thalatta is one of my fondest memories from my school days, as a 13 year old this was my first time away from home without my parents and hence was particularly exciting and a brand new experience. In fact there were so many brand new experiences that week, which included: sleeping in hammock s, cooking and washing up! No one checking up on you to make sure that you cleaned your teeth (but I did anyway), and of course just being at sea, helping to sail the thing. The sails were coated in some vile red protective coating and pulling them up and down the masts and rolling them up made your hands and pretty much the rest of you the same colour as the sails because it rubbed off on anything that got close to it . Pulling on ropes and winding the windlasses was also pretty exhausting but great fun, not so great when it was raining and blowing what seemed like a small gale but on the whole brilliant . I also recall that the school made a big play about being invited to go on the trip. I'm not sure what the selection criteria was or who made the decision as to who got to go but I'm glad I was one of the few who did."
John Wilson

Moving on nearly a decade we are lucky enough to be able to get another taste of life on board. Catharine Lockwood has very kindly supplied the following account of a trip which she made made in early 1983, we think it gives a first rate flavour of a trip at that time.

Southend High School for Girls Thalatta Trip 4th-8th April 1983

The group was divided into two watches as follows;

"Ticks"	"Tocks"
Sally Castle	Tania Griffin
Catherine Lockwood	Tracy Longhurst
Lisa Masterson	Fleur Oates
Lisa McAllister	Lianne Oulten
Joanne Roxburgh	Fiona Philpott
Margaret Torkington	Philippa Wilson

Day 1

The afternoon of Monday 4th April 1983 was quite sunny, as twelve of us gradually arrived at the Town Quay at Maldon. When we were all there, Miss Benham showed us and our parents aboard and we all made a bee-line for the hammocks, finding one to sleep in. Our parents were told various things about the barge, and shown the place where we were to sleep, and we then got rid of them.

Miss Benham then proceeded to tell us how everything worked, and much to our dismay, everything was operated by pumps! There was a pump for the toilet, washbasin, and 2 for the sink" We were also left to experiment with our hammocks. I will say no more.

While we were still below, the engine was started and we all put on our life jackets and clambered up the hatch which was rather narrow, and found ourselves in the process of manoeuvring out of Maldon from the Town Quay. This was made awkward by the fact that there was another barge on the berth outside us, and it had to move down river while the "Thalatta" turned slowly round. When we went down the river, the other barge ("Convoy") went back to the Quay.

At 4.00pm the topsail, foresail and half the mainsail were raised, and we soon realized that we had paid money to have a holiday which was designed to kill! It also got quite cold, so we went below and put on jumpers, wellies, coats, gloves, and HATS!

As we went down river, we passed the barge "Reminder" which was on its way to Maldon. At 4.30pm the rest of the mainsail was set. We passed Heybridge and then came up to Osea Island. There are two ways round this island. The main channel runs to the South, and to the North, there is no channel, but at low tide it dries out completely to reveal a road from the mainland to Osea. At high tide, this way is only about 6 ft deep. We went to the North, and "Thalatta" is the only barge that does that.

As we got behind the island, the South Westerly wind which had been blowing well, dropped completely, and so to speed us up, the engine was started, and the foresail was lowered, and also, some brave people managed to brail the mainsail at about 5.45. At about 6.00, we passed Bradwell and the Nuclear Power Station. Anchored just off Bradwell are quite a few big ships which are not being used because there is no work and there are no places for them to moor in London.

We anchored not long after, just off West Mersea for the night. In the evening, we had our meal and wrote up our logs for the day, before fighting the hammocks. In the night it rained hard.

Day 2

We woke up early, in fact it was about 4.30 when most of us were awakened by the bumping of the ship's boats against the side of the barge, also a few people were talking quietly. As it was impossible to go to sleep again, we all just lay in our hammocks talking. Then, at 7.30, Miss Benham came in and told us that it was time to get up, and also told us where they hoped to take us for the day. We were to go out of the River Blackwater, and go up the coast, and through Harwich Harbour, and up the River Orwell to Pin Mill.

We all noticed, when we got up, that the South Westerly wind was decidedly stronger, and most stomachs felt this during or after breakfast! While one group, the "ticks", stayed below to attempt to cook a breakfast of bacon and eggs, the other group, the "tocks", went on deck to polish the brass.

At 9.30, it was time to be off, so while a few of us winched in the anchor, the rest hauled up the topsail, mainsail, foresail and mizzen. We thought that was all the hard work, but no, we had to haul both the ship's boats up into the davits and that was terribly hard!

As we passed Bradwell and the rest of the ships, the little chapel on the sea wall became clear. We also passed the mouth of the River Colne and then entered the Wallet. A little way away, there was another barge which was going through the Whitaker channel. Between "Thalatta" and this other barge was a dangerous sandbank. Sandbanks are marked by buoys which are different shapes and colours

The channel which we went through – The Wallet – used to be frequented by pirate radio ships which used to broadcast just outside the three-mile boundary in the sixties.

At 10:55, the foresail was lowered. Then, Miss Benham presented us with two empty bottles, and suggested that we should put a message in each, from the groups, and hope that someone would answer it. So each group was given a bottle and a piece of paper and put their heads together to sort out a super message. After a photo session, the two bottles were thrown into the sea, somewhere off Clacton. Then the mainsail and mizzen were both brailed.

At 12:00, we entered Harwich Harbour having passed Clacton, Frinton and Walton. In Harwich, there are two lighthouses. Before buoys were invented, the only safe way of getting into the harbour without hitting a sandbank, was by putting the two lighthouses in line with each other. Nowadays, one is a council house, and the other is a maritime museum.

Opposite Harwich is Felixstowe which is a fast growing port which offers employment to more people than any other port. Just off Felixstowe is the place where the "European Gateway" sank. She was raised just the week before we were there.

It was a relief to get into the sheltered waters of the River Orwell. There are two rivers, which, at their meeting point form Harwich Harbour. They are the Stour and the Orwell. We went up the Orwell because the South East wind which was forecast would have provided some rough water, and the Orwell was sheltered.

We anchored in Butterman's Bay at 2.40 and then waited until the tide had risen a bit, and then at 4.00, we clambered into one of the ship's boats and the skipper took us ashore. We landed by Clamp House and so we had to walk through the woods to Pin Mill, and then up a lane to Chelmondiston where we bought some food and sweets. All the time, it poured with rain and we got soaked to the skin. We then had to walk back to Pin Mill and then waited for 15 minutes until at 6.00 we were picked up by both the skipper and Miss Benham in both the boats.

By the time we got back to the "Thalatta" we were frozen and so the fire was put on to dry our clothes. We had some soup to warm us up and then we got on with writing our logs while a few got on with making the evening meal. It wasn't ready until 9.15!!!!! Obviously "lights out" had to be suspended, and when we eventually got into our hammocks it was 10.00.

Day 3

We got more sleep in the night, although Joanne managed to fall out of her hammock. We woke up at 7.30, and Miss Benham gave us an extra half hour before coming to get us out at 8.00. Our group, the "ticks", went on deck at 8.35 and polished the brass on the deck while the "tocks" made the breakfast, which we ate at 9.20.

At 10.00 the anchor was winched in, and the "tocks" hauled up the foresail, half mainsail, topsail and mizzen. We went back down the River Orwell. At 10.30 the rest of the mainsail was set.

At 11.30, while most were below eating "elevenses", a few brave ones were braving the cold South Westerly wind as we went through Harwich Harbour. The engine was put on so that we would get through the harbour quickly without getting in the way of any large ships which could run us down. Then, it was turned off at 12.15, only to be turned on again at 12.30. At 12.35, the foresail was lowered, and the mizzen and mainsail were both brailed.

We tacked back down he coast. This was because as we couldn't go straight into the wind, we kept changing course, in a zig-zag movement.

We passed Walton, Clacton and Frinton and narrowly avoided being soaked by two squalls. We rounded Colne Point, and went into the River Colne where we anchored at 3.30 off East Mersea.

At 4.00, we clambered into the ships boat and the skipper took us ashore to East Mersea along with an orange football. The game of football gradually turned into rugby, and then into rounders, which had to stop when we saw lightning and heard thunder.

When it started to rain, some went to shelter in an old pill-box and soon came back complaining that it smelt. So we all went back to the shore and a few girls started questioning a fisherman about his hobby and what sort of fish he caught because we had all been given a project to do. Then we watched "Thalatta" to see if anyone would rescue us, and sure enough, when someone appeared on deck we waved and were noticed, and duly rescued.

When we got back, wet clothes were dried, and dinner was made – earlier than the night before! We did our logs, or at least some did, because there was washing-up to be done.

Lights out was at the usual time of 9.30.

Day 4

We woke up at 7.30 and Miss Benham came in at 8.00 and told us what we would be doing that day. When we had managed to get out of our hammocks and get dressed, the "tocks" went on deck while the "ticks" prepared breakfast – scrambled eggs.

At 10.00, we clambered into the ships boats and were taken ashore to Brightlingsea. As we went towards the slipway where we were to land, we saw a sailing ship moored up outside a boat yard, and this was the "Soren Larsen", the ship used in the "Onedin Line". We then walked up the roads towards the high street – our first contact with civilization for 4 whole days! We went in all the food shops in our efforts to find grub for the party in the evening, and Miss Benham got some sherry for our trifle.

We went back to the slipway at about 11.15 (my legs had got so used to being on a rocking ship that I kept swaying about and walking into things!) and then got into the boats and made our way back to the barge. The "tocks" made dinner, sandwiches and soup, straight away.

After this, the "tocks" went on deck to haul up the anchor while us "ticks" stayed below to do the washing-up. The engine was put on at 2.10, and we left the River Colne, rounded Mersea and went into the River Blackwater where we passed several big ships:-"Aliakmon River", "Zak", "Cape Avanti", "Due", "Essex Ferry" and "Norfolk Ferry".

We passed Bradwell at 3.15 and carried on up river and passed the Stone at St Lawrence at 4.00. As we came up to Osea Island, we could see Anthony Wedgewood Benn's house on the mainland and we then anchored just off Osea.

Then came the fun, because both teams were given a side of the decks of the barge to scrub and so the full kit of oilskins was put on, and we set to work with four people in each group armed with brushes, and the other two were pumping the seawater in and pointing the hose at the deck. By the time we had finished, there wasn't a speck of dirt to be seen anywhere!

After this, we had our party. Lots of food had been prepared, and all of it went, including the trifle of which there were seconds and thirds for everyone. Miss Benham donated half a bottle of white wine as well.

When it came to cutting the cake, the skipper was invited down to officiate, and he complimented the cook by saying that the decoration on the top looked like coniferous trees on a hillside – it was meant to be "Thalatta"! After our meal we went up on deck for a while until it got too cold, and we went to bed straight away as we were very tired, and full.

Day 5

We woke up at 5.30 and were roused out of our hammocks at 7.30. None of us had any breakfast because we had all overeaten the night before. Cleaning and scrubbing soon got under way as everything had to be ready for the next group – which were from Shoebury. Also, the ship's newspaper was written for the skipper.

At 9.05, four of us plus Miss Benham hauled up the anchor and the engine was put on. We motored upriver towards Maldon. We were going to get there earlier than our disembarkation time because the tide had to be high for "Thalatta" to get in at Maldon. On our way up, we passed another barge called "Reminder" which was starting on a painting/birdwatching trip, and Miss Matson was on board, so we all went up on deck to wave.

When we arrived at Maldon, at 10.30, "Thalatta" had a job to get in because the stern of a boat called "Kenya Jacaranda" was sticking out, and all the other barges had to move up to make room for her.

Our parents soon began to arrive, so at 10.40 we were given half hour shore leave, and we all plodded up the High Street and some got chocolates which were given to Miss Benham and the skipper (who had disappeared) should also have been there too. Then, after a photo-session, we went below to collect all our gear and to make sure nothing was left behind (I managed to leave a pair of old gloves in my oilskins by mistake). Then we said thank you to Miss Benham and clambered over the two barges on the inside berths and met our parents. We all hoped that we would have another chance to go on "Thalatta" as we had had a marvellous time!

Cathy Curtis
    (nee Catherine Lockwood)

Chapter Six
Rita's Story

Moving forward two decades or so, Rita was third hand on board *Thalatta* for the five years before her renovation. In this diary written in 2005, she recalls a typical week.

Monday, early in April

Today sees us all arrive bright and early at the quay side. Kevin, the skipper, helps me stow the stores which my husband and I have purchased over the weekend. Tinned food and cereals go in the cupboard next to the galley, frozen items in the fridge and fresh fruit and vegetables in the little storage area in the Focs'l.

No sooner are we finished than this week's group arrives. They are from a prep school in Surrey and have had an "interesting" journey round the M25. This group is a mixed bunch of excited nine and ten year olds, which makes settling in and briefings great fun!

With all their personal kit stowed in big wooden lockers below their hammocks it is time for our new young crew to listen attentively to the safety briefing. The briefing covers such things as not running, always wearing life jackets on deck, where it is and is not safe to be when we are sailing and so on. Oh yes, and that the skippers word is law!

Boxes and Hammocks

As usual there is much excitement at the prospect of climbing into and not falling out the hammocks. I am firm, no one is allowed to try them out until bed time!

With formalities completed, we cast off from the quay motoring up to Osea Island before Roger, our mate, lets out the anchor.

At Osea Island we have lunch, the children having brought sandwiches for this first meal. I do however prepare something for the crew.

After lunch we motor our way down the River Blackwater before hoisting the sails to take advantage of some decent sailing weather.

As we are passing Bradwell Power Station, a Porpoise joins us briefly, much to everybody's delight, mine especially as I have never seen one before. After too brief a time our companion disappears and we are all left with just a unique memory.

We sail our way to Brightlingsea, where we anchor for the evening. It is then the usual first night routine of logbook completion and hammock boarding instruction! When everyone has settled down I go up on deck to ring my husband, Peter.

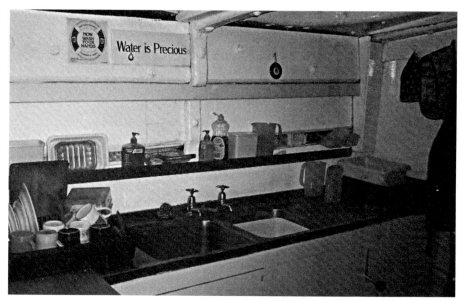

The Galley

Tuesday

Today we are up and away early. We use the engine to come out of Brightlingsea, which gives us a brief view of its hilltop Church of All Saints, with its display of tiles in the Nave, a memorial to all the local men lost at sea, including one who went down with the Titanic. It is perhaps no bad thing to occasionally be reminded that there can be a price to be paid by those who work on the water.

We continue to motor on past St. Osyth, though we can see nothing of the vast 12th Century Abbey known as the Priory. We pass Clacton and up to Walton on the Naze. Here we hoist the Fors'l, tops'l and part of the mains'l ready to Sail into Walton Backwaters.

By lunchtime we are safely anchored in the Backwaters so Roger and our skipper Kevin are able to take the group ashore in one of the dinghies. The youngsters and the teacher enjoy themselves playing on the beach while our "Boys" dig for lugworms to use as bait for the evenings fishing. Fishing seems, one way or another, to feature quite prominently on Thalatta!

All proceeds smoothly for the afternoon as the group returns from a good afternoon ashore and Roger and Kevin have a plentiful supply of bait, sufficient that, after dinner, the crabbing and fishing are enjoyed by our crew, young and not so young alike.

Wednesday

After breakfast Kevin and Roger take everyone ashore to visit Walton. Roger stays ashore with the group while Kevin brings both dinghies back to the barge. Meanwhile, I busy myself in the galley making sandwiches ready for lunch.

Before long Kevin goes ashore once more to collect the group who now have with them young Andrew who is joining us late having been ill for the start of the trip.

By 13.00 we are all able to enjoy our lunch on deck while enjoying glorious sunshine - bliss! After lunch it's up with the anchor, set the sails and head towards Harwich and Felixstowe.

As I watch Walton slowly disappear behind us, I am reminded of a hot summers afternoon the previous year.

There we were motoring along quite nicely as we made our way to Walton Backwaters to anchor for the night as we so often do. It was a lovely afternoon as most are on board when the sun is shining and the *kids are happy. I see that a group of the children are standing by the Port rail looking across at the Naze.*

Even from here, we can see quite clearly the effects of soil erosion as parts of the cliffs have slid untidily down onto the beach. The green of stranded turf speckled on the red London clay clearly indicating the freshness of the damage.

Roger is explaining some of the history of the area. Pointing out the Octagonal Naze Tower, rising over eighty feet from the cliff top, it would be easy for him just to tell his audience that in 1720 it was built for Trinity House to act as a marker for ships making for Harwich harbor. Easy, yes. Characteristic? No.

"Can you see that tall red building over there?" He asks his young listeners.

"Yes" they obligingly reply, presenting the opportunity he has been waiting for.

"You know that the soil erosion round here is very bad don't you?" Some heads nod in agreement, someone asks what "erosion" means.

"Erosion means that the wind and the sea wear away the soil so that the land starts falling into the water, like those cliffs over there"

By now of course he has the audience in the palm of his hand.

"That was built nearly three hundred years ago," He says pointing to the tower, "but in those days it was a WELL!"

I try to hide my amusement while perhaps thinking that The Naze Tower has had a busy enough life, serving as look out post, radio mast platform and Radar site as well as its original function, without having to do duty as a well!

To his credit, Roger reverts to "Real" history when he relates,

"The original village of Walton is a long way from here. In fact, it is about nine miles out to sea! The village church was one of the last buildings left and that fell into the sea in 1798!"

By this time, I am not sure if anybody believes him! I know he is telling the truth when he tells of the areas connection with Admiral the Lord Nelson.

"In August 1801, Nelson was checking the coastal fortifications around Harwich when word arrived that Napoleon's French fleet was preparing to set out to invade England. Nelson was now desperate to get back to the Thames Estuary to take command of his own fleet.

The Medusa, a thirty-two gun Frigate was anchored off shore, ready to sail. Speed is vital if Nelson is to get back in time to save England! Every minute is vital on the long voyage south with the Nations fate at stake!

There is a shortcut, a hazardous inshore passage, which will save precious hours sailing out to the east of offshore sandbanks. The local Maritime Pilots declared that it was far too dangerous to take a ship the size of a Frigate that way.

Despite these warnings Nelson had the courage, and good fortune, to find a local maritime surveyor who new the passage well enough to guide them through the shallow waters of Walton Flats. Running close under the tower, Medusa sped towards the waiting fleet and destiny!

This daring piece of seamanship which helped to save England gave a name to that stretch of water still known today as "The Medusa Channel" after the frigate".

Reverie over it is time to return to the present. This evening, two of the boys, Jamie and Andrew help me to prepare our meal of pizza and salad followed by strawberry cheesecake.

Thursday

We are up early so that we can wind up the anchor before breakfast!

Coming out into the channel as we leave Shotley where we have spent the night the sea becomes very choppy and Roger is concerned for me. I am organising the children washing up when he comes below, sending me up on deck where I will be less susceptible to seasickness.

Fortunately however this is one malady with which I do not suffer though I take the chance of enjoying a few minutes of the wind and spray in my face. Not something I get a lot of in the galley!

We make our way back past Walton, Clacton and Brightlingsea without stopping, as the weather is too rough here to take the boats ashore comfortably.

We are able to drop anchor at Osea Island, in the Blackwater, when we get there as the wind has now dropped and it is nice enough for us to go ashore so that we can picnic on the beach. Later, most of the children go paddling, Alexandra and Tim however are adventurous (Daft?) and brave the April temperatures to have a swim. While this is going on Kevin and Roger organise a tug of war between Port and Starboard watches, which gives rise to much hilarity, and amid which Starboard watch wins, we think!

It is not long before our intrepid swimmers decide that it is much more fun, and warmer, playing on the beach. I think they are especially glad when by late afternoon it is time to go back on board for hot drinks all round. Everybody appreciated this refreshment, not least those members of the crew who are not as young as others.

Tonight, Alexandra and Emily prepare the dinner and we all enjoy their lasagne, peas and mash, despite the fact that we ran out of gas half way through the meal and the bottle had to be replaced. Try finding that in a cookbook! Afterwards some of the children purchase their gifts from our shop and most do some crabbing before Kevin gives his evening talk

Friday

Today's first job is to make our way the short distance back to Maldon while the children prepare for their return home. They all have their bags packed and up on deck by 11.00 then its time for them to sweep up the hold and check all the boxes to make sure that nothing is left behind.   Once everything is tidy the hammocks are turned upside down so that no dust, sand, socks or stray crabs are left in them!

The group has its lunch up on deck, just before we arrive at the quay. When we arrive, we have to wait for the Alice (Now based at Portsmouth) to move so that we can use her berth. All is settled and the group gets ashore by 13.30 so then its time for a final tidy up before I leave for home".

Thalatta safely tied up at Maldon for the weekend

Chapter Seven
Kidnapping

It is not just young people who have reaped great benefits from time spent sailing *Thalatta*. In the years immediately preceding her refurbishment ECST regularly linked up with the Odyssey Organisation and the Chaucer Hospital in Kent to provide trips for patients in remission from various forms of cancer.

It is the philosophy of Odyssey to use the stimulations of surprise and the great outdoors to combat the psychological and emotional devastation caused by the disease.

To achieve these objectives Odyssey seeks out wild and peaceful places, steeped in atmosphere, where people have the chance to try activities they may never have tried before. These can include orienteering, gliding and of course, working on a Thames sailing barge.

It is part of the philosophy of adventure on these courses that the people involved should have only a limited knowledge of what lies ahead!

Your authors were privileged to be on one of these trips in a glorious summers week in 2003. We would like to give you just a hint of what it was like and to quote from the notes we made at the time.

We anchored in Oare Creek , near Faversham in Kent. The plan was that we would take on one group of twelve people for two days then swap them for another group for the rest of the week. Simple really, except that of course the people concerned did not know where they were going or what they were going to do!

A warm and sunny morning saw skipper Kevin and mate Roger disappear in one of the ships boats, to return shortly afterwards with all the party's luggage. That was the easy bit! Getting twelve people on board without them knowing what was going on would be slightly more difficult.

With time to spare until collecting our charges, we enjoyed a leisurely lunch at the splendid Shipwright's Arms before returning to Thalatta to wait.

Our genuine "state of the art" skipper and mate returned to the shore in readiness for our party, while two "cardboard cut out" crew members (Rita and Peter) remained on board.

As previously cunningly planned with the groups leader/organiser, Kevin and Roger were casually gossiping by the ships boats at the waters edge when our unsuspecting victims happened along.

The ensuing conversation would probably gone something along these lines;

Group leader "Hi, can you tell us anything about that funny looking boat out there?"

Roger   "Yes, she is a Thames sailing barge"

G.L.   "Oh, that's interesting, can you tell us anything about her?" (innocently)

Roger   "Well, if you have got a few minutes we can do better than that, would you like to go for a sail round her?"

G,L (After consulting the now enthusiastic group) "Yes please" - Hook Line and Sinker!

The two ships boats, Jane and John are duly loaded with people and make their way over to Thalatta. Much chatter ensues on the trip with everyone being encouraged to be curious about this fine old sailing ship riding at anchor in the evening sunlight.

Arriving alongside our devious duo hail the two "Sailors" idling on deck.

"Hi do you mind us having a look at your ship?"

"No, of course not. Would you like to come aboard?"

Further consultation takes place on the smaller vessels, Kevin and Roger let it be known that they "Just about have enough time."

One by one, some confidently, some hesitantly twelve ladies come on board staring wide eyed at this glamorous old sailing ship. Oddly as it may seem to our visitors, it is the two eager boatmen rather than the "Crew" who start to show them round.

Understanding slowly starts to dawn until after a few minutes Kevin announces

"OK ladies, this is where you are going to spend the next two days, you will be sailing our barge"

Whilst it is perhaps fair to say that this statement is greeted with varying degrees of enthusiasm, it is not long before everyone settles down to enjoy the next stage of their adventure.

One of the benefits of these trips is the re learning of self reliance and building back up of self confidence. As part of this our ladies took over the galley cooking for themselves while the regular crew fended for themselves using the small galley in the focs'l.

A full account of this trip, can be found in *The Thalatta Diaries* from Heritage House (Publishing) Ltd. However, suffice to say here that a VERY good time was had by all and the sheer joy of living and enthusiasm for everything shown by the girls was infectious.

We would now like to share something of what these trips could mean to those involved. What follows was written the year after *Thalatta* was dry docked.

We were so moved that we put down our thoughts at the time in case such a book as this should ever be written. We have not edited the original text which was of course, written before Eunice passed away a few months later.

"Rita and I were surprised when one morning the post brought something other than a circular or a bill. Even more surprising was that this unexpected letter was an invitation to a Birthday party being thrown for Eunice, the sister of Hilary a friend of Rita's.

Eunice had been on one of the Chaucer trips on the Thalatta two years ago and had been so impressed that apparently she has never stopped talking about it! Through Hilary, who lives locally, Eunice had bought a copy of The Thalatta Diaries and thoroughly enjoyed the read. (Obviously has taste!)

Eunice now resides in The Heart of Kent hospice just outside Maidstone. It had been decided to throw a big Birthday party for her, inviting as many family and friends as possible. Rita had been invited because of the affection with which Eunice remembered her and the rest of the crew of Thalatta when she had what she described as one of the "Best times of my life".

Thus it was with mixed emotions that Rita and I made the long trek down the various motorways, across the Q.E.ll Bridge and into the wilds of Kent (well the M20 anyway!)

When we arrived we were pleased that although windy, the weather was dry and sunny with enough warmth to allow Eunice to greet her guests from her wheelchair on the patio in front of the main building. As well as several young children, a pet dog also played happily around the chairs wheels until guided into a pen for safety's sake.

The hospice looked to provide a cheery and stimulating environment without the "Hospital atmosphere" which I had feared.

All things considered Eunice looked well and it was pleasing that despite us having been warned that it might not be the case, she remembered Rita and the crew and was able to chat for a few minutes, reminiscing about her time on board the Thalatta.

We were able to tell Eunice about the rebuild Thalatta is now undergoing in dry dock at St.Osyth and the hopes that we have for the future of the work of the barge.

We spent a pleasant hour or more talking to other guests before the Birthday cake was brought in for Eunice to duly blow out, with the help of one of the younger guests.

We eventually deemed it time to leave Eunice in the company of her family but not before having one last chat about life on the barge and presenting her with some pictures of "The Old Girl" in dry dock.

All in all an afternoon which, for us at least, very much served to put into perspective the work done by The East Coast Sail Trust".

A passage that to us reflects the real value of vessels like *Thalatta* and the work they continue to do.

Thalatta at anchor

Chapter Eight
Day Sails

One important way of raising revenue in support of *Thalatta* and the East Coast Sail Trust is by day excursions or "Day Sails" where supporters can book a cruise for the day at preferential rates. Besides being important for raising money, they also happen to be darn good fun!

The following account was written for the excellent *Tollesbury Parish Magazine* just before *Thalatta* came out of the water.

"It's that time of year again! The time of year when I evade work for the day and "help" my wife, Rita on board the Thames Sailing Barge Thalatta.

Thalatta is a hundred-year (nearly) old barge owned by the East Coast Sail Trust, based at Maldon in Essex. She normally earns her living by giving Monday to Friday educational trips to school groups. This week however she is raising much-needed funds by giving day trips to adults from Ipswich docks.

Rita's job is to be in charge of the galley and below deck area when the barge is at sea. This involves responsibility for the weekly provisioning and for organising the youngsters in their cooking duties.

For Day Sails she has the more mundane duty of keeping all of our guest crew suitably fed and watered from stores supplied by an outside caterer. This generates a lot of washing up, that's where I come in!

Now, on with the story. We arrive bright and early at Ipswich dock, park and take a leisurely stroll to the pontoon where Thalatta dutifully waits for us ninety foot of black hulled and blue decked barge, the traditional colours going back to when he was built in 1906.

We pause briefly to admire the "Pickle" moored on the other side of the dock. This "Pickle" is a replica of the small vessel, which brought the first news of Nelson's victory to these shores two hundred years ago and is at Ipswich as part of the Trafalgar Day celebrations.

Once we reach Thalatta we climb the steps that take us up the side of her oak hull and step onto the colourful deck. On board we are greeted by a cheery "Mornin' Rita" "How you doin' Pete?" From Cyril, our skipper. Cyril is a contagiously cheerful, bearded sort who would not look out of place in a pirate film.

Once aboard the first job is to get the huge iron kettle onto the gas stove in the galley ready for the first brew of the day. That will be tea for the crew.

The "Pickle" replica

There is still plenty of time until our guests arrive so we grab a few minutes of relaxation while we enjoy our drinks. Just as we finish, Joe Brannigan, the Chairman of the East Coast Sail Trust arrives, followed shortly by the caterers with our supplies for the day. These arrive in three large white polystyrene boxes, which have to be passed up from the pontoon to the deck. Reaching over the side I am very careful how I take these large and awkward containers as to drop one, spilling its contents in the water would only remain funny for a fraction of a second!

Supplies safely on deck we now manhandle them down the steep narrow companionway that leads into the hold. Once used for carrying everything from malt to coal, the hold now serves as the main living and dining area for school and adult crews alike.

An enormous wooden dining table and the dozen wooden sea chests, which serve to store our young crew's gear when they are at sea for the week, dominate this area.

Once everything is below we make our way forward, ducking hammocks as we go, finally storing the food in the cabin that serves as accommodation for the Leader on the school trips. The children, much to their delight, sleep in the afore mentioned hammocks!

46

Back up on deck, we greet the first of our passengers for the day. Over the next few minutes all of our day-trippers arrive to be welcomed aboard by Joe and to be served tea and coffee by Rita and me.

Before we can set sail however, Cyril assembles everyone on deck for the safety briefing. We all sit around listening intently, not only because in the unlikely event of an emergency this could save lives but also because our skipper usually makes it entertaining!

As usual the briefing starts with an apology for talking to everyone as though they are twelve years old. This, Cyril explains, is because most of the people he gives the briefing to are that age!

We receive careful instruction, among other things on the use of the life jackets. We are told that they self inflate on contact with the water, we also told what to do if they do not inflate (manual operation of gas bottle) and if they still do not inflate (blow hard down the tube). We also get the crack about taking it back if it still does not work. This joke, usually applied to parachutes, is older than anyone on board!

Cyril is most specific about what to do if anyone goes overboard. Loud call of "Man overboard", point and keep pointing to the person in the water even if you do look like a demented Darlek!

We are also warned to stay clear of the danger areas when the sails are up. In their days in trade more than one unfortunate crewman was lost overboard when a barge has gybed and the mains'l and sheet block have swept across the horse taking all before them. This has never happened on Thalatta and we do not intend to start now.

Safety briefing complete, our day sail crew make themselves comfortable around the deck. The weather is now warming up in the pleasant September sunshine as Rita and I make our down to the galley to finish the washing up and put the kettle on for mid morning coffee.

Chores temporarily complete we surface once more just as we begin the process of "locking out" of Ipswich port. We have made the short journey thus far under the power of our big Kalvin diesel with the slight whiff of exhaust and its slow revving dumpa, dumpa, dumpa, reminding us that we are not, despite any evidence to the contrary, still in the early Twentieth Century. Once in the confines of the lock, Cyril nudges the barge up close to the starboard side while Roger makes fast with the ropes, which will keep us steady. "Hold tight now, here we go!" Warns the lock keeper over his Tannoy. With this we notice the sides of the lock getting higher as the water level subsides to that of the river outside. Soon the big iron lock gates swing open to release us to continue our journey, encourages by a cheery "OK folks, have a good trip" from the lock keeper.

We make our way, past the assorted vessels lining the Ipswich riverside. The Motor Vessel Harmony, resplendent in a seemingly new coat of blue paint. said to be in preparation for a new life as a floating showroom for a furniture company, perhaps she may yet visit exotic destinations!

Rita and I make our way below as it is now time to serve elevenses. While below everything goes quiet as Cyril exchanges engine for sail power. Our day sail crew, we know, are being put to work holding this and hauling that getting the sail raised and the deck tidy.

It is not long before we bring up the coffee and tea and join the others sitting on the hatch, with its brass work glinting in the sun having been polished by Cyril and I while we were waiting for the others to board! Cyril is a total enthusiast and happy to do the most menial of jobs to keep Thalatta looking in top condition.

Our Day Sail crew relax and Rita stretches her legs on deck

We gently make our way by Woolverstone Marina, our home for day sails in recent years, but now too full for sailing barges to use C y r i l has set only our tops'l so things remain calm while we take our refreshments. However when these are finished its all volunteers to work putting up the main and fors'l and down below we notice a decided lean as we pick up speed!

We make our way out past "Cat House" (allegedly so called because of the shape of a cat which used to be displayed in the window to warn of the presence of Revenue Men.) and past the magnificent vista of the Ipswich School looking down on us from the south bank of the Orwell.

Three years ago, Rita and I had the pleasure of attending Cyril's wedding reception at that school and can vouch for its splendid situation and views over the river.

While collecting crockery on deck ready for washing up I hear another barge has been sighted. Sure enough we see the Xylonite bearing down on us from the Felixstowe direction. Now it is time for action, I watch as water balloons are brought on deck and our main armament prepared, "The Funnaliser", a bucket attached to bungee cords attached to the rigging!

The barges close at a seemingly alarming rate! (Well, maybe twelve knots!) As we pass each other water balloons are hurled and the Funnaliser unleashed. I would like to say that Xylonites' rapid disappearance was due to a wish to avoid our bombardment. Sadly I have to report that our highly trained crew missed with everything!

Returning below we find that the magnificent sailing conditions and the consequent excitement we have had on deck has, like all good things, to be paid for. The angle at which we are sailing has allowed water to seep from the bilge into the hold. A few minutes mopping and drying and all is ship shape again. Bilge pumps definitely on now however!

All on board settle down to enjoy the sailing, making our way down to Felixstowe where we can admire the hundreds of multi coloured containers which decorate the docks. We can also admire the many and various craft moored around, including retired light ships in their red paint looking like so many nautical Santa's.

It is now time for Rita and I to lay out the table and serve lunch, making sure of course that the skipper is provided for. This is an essential duty since Cyril likes to continue sailing during the meal so cannot leave the wheel!

Joe, the East Coast Sail Trust Chairman serves wine and our guest crew sits down to a fine repast. Such fare contrasts with the somewhat more frugal meals they may have had to endure if they were a working crew when the barge was "In trade", especially if there were few cargoes to be had! "Starvation" buoys were not so called in jest.

When the meal is eventually complete Cyril and Roger get everyone organised on deck. More work for those so inclined or sunbathing for those who are not! I am however now consigned to the galley to do the washing up!

Washing up in Thalatta's galley means first boiling our great kettle on the gas stove then filling two bowls with water. One bowl is used to pre wash plates, the other to give them their final wash. There is not water to spare on a barge to keep replenishing the washing up bowl.

When we have finished below there is just enough time to come up on deck (checking we are not about to gybe before emerging from the companionway, don't want to lose our heads)! By now we are making our way, still under sail, back up towards the docks. An all too brief sunbathe before it is time to set out afternoon teas, this is not a trip for those on a diet!

By the time we have served and consumed afternoon tea it is time for our more energetic colleagues to be coerced into doing some more work. That is, helping to take down the sails.

We pass Pin Mill, once a smugglers haven, now renown for its pleasure sailing and as the home of the 17th Century Butt and Oyster pub.

Bird watchers amongst us are rewarded with sights of Little Terns, Cormorants and Herons to name but some of the wildlife on view.

All too soon the sails are down and the engine starts its rhythmical beat as we make our way once more into the lock. We here once more the lock keepers well practiced liturgy of "Hold tight" and "here we go then" followed once more by a cheery fare well.

Once through the lock we make our way back towards our berth, past the new residential developments, rumored to be fetching half a million pounds per flat. Some of us observe that we would be prepared to pay an awful lot of money NOT to live there!

Finally we are ready to maneuver into position to tie up. Roger bravely stations me at the stern with the tyre on a rope which acts as a fender to protect our wooden hull against the corner of the pontoon as we nestle in position. I am given strict instructions to "Stay out of my way" as he makes fast the lines!

With great dexterity (who am I kidding?) I just about manage to stay out of Roger's way, and lasso the pontoon corner with the tyre. This latter was not what was supposed to happen but since we manage to tie up OK without getting any holes in our hull all seems to be well.

Sadly it is now time for farewells as our day sailors make there way ashore. After a brief tidy up Rita and I also say our goodbyes for the day and make our way home".

Approaching the Orwell Bridge on the way back

Chapter Nine
From the children's logs

The children who come on board probably deserve to have the last word on a tip on *Thalatta* at this time.

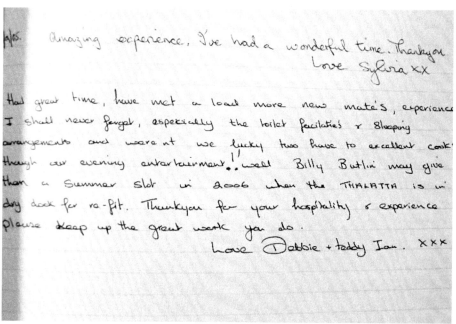

The log entry reads;

13/9/2005 *Amazing experience I've had a wonderful time, thank you.*

Love Silvia XX

Had great time, have met a load more new mates, experience I shall never forget, especially the toilet facilities and sleeping arrangements and weren't we lucky two have to excellent cooks though our evening's entertainment! Well Billy Butlin may give them a summer slot in 2006 when the Thalatta is in dry dock for a re fit. Thank you for your hospitality and experience. Please keep up the great work you do.

Love Debbie and Teddy, Ian xxx

The following page has two pictures drawn by members of school groups. The first sums up the most memorable parts of a trip for the artist-crabbing, cooking, talking, and always popular, sleeping in hammocks!

The second picture is one of our all time favourites. Drawn by a young man from a school specialising in Special Educational Needs, the alternative view of life is titled *"Crabs peopling"*.

The world of Thalatta summed up in a single picture by one artist and, below the simply brilliant - Crabs peopling!

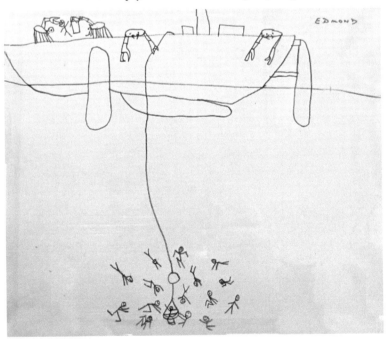

Chapter Ten
A new beginning

Even the best built and cared for vessels eventual reach a stage where the ravages of time and hard use start to take their toll.

Over the years inevitably routine maintenance was not always sufficient to keep the old lady in first class condition. A new transom was fitted one year, major work to the rudder post followed. As time went by, a small but persistent leak worsened.

As *Thalatta* approached her centenary it became apparent that much would need to be done if she was to survive her second hundred years.

Thus it was that when the BBC and other local media carried an announcement in April 2005 stating that the Heritage Lottery Fund (HLF) had made a grant to East Coast Sail Trust for work to be carried out on *Thalatta*. This was not as a result of a sudden whim but the culmination of months, if not years of hard work preparing a suitable application.

That this application succeeded where many have failed was due in no small part to the attention to detail and diligence of Nick Hayward who took on this vital task in the role of an adviser to the Trustees.

The original estimate of the cost of carrying out restoration work on *Thalatta* was £792,000 of which HLF agreed to grant 66,55% or £527,500, with the ECST finding the rest in Matching Funding. The grant was not without strings however and a Mortgage Covenant Agreement with extensive conditions was required.

Raising the money for the restoration of a Thames sailing barge is only ever part of the problem in this day and age, neither the facilities nor the expertise are as widely available as they were a century ago!

After some deliberation, Andy Harman's St Osyth Boatyard on the East Essex coast was chosen, having both the expertise and facilities courtesy of many years working on wooden vessels. Andy is also well known as a highly successful Thames Barge Match competitor in his barge *Edme,* one of the few to still operate by sail alone, never having been fitted with an engine.

It was on a cold, wintry March day in 2006 that Gary Diddams, Technical adviser to the ECST and former skipper of *Thalatta* set out with Ruth, his fiancée (now wife) together with Roger Davies as mate to bring the barge from Maldon to her new home at the boatyard. With tides necessitating an overnight trip and with heavy snow showers during the voyage, it was perhaps not the most comfortable journey the crew would ever have made. The weather was not finished with *Thalatta* when she arrived at St. Osyth. Mooring and lowering masts and rigging are made so much more interesting when combined with heavy snow!

Safely settled into her new home, *Thalatta* started her rejuvenation. Everything possible was taken off and stored, either into a large container or in the yard. It was necessary to make the vessel as light as possible before putting her into dry dock (also known as "the Pontoon") as there is not a great depth of water at St.Osyth even on a high tide. Preparations complete, the next suitable tide saw *Thalatta* floated into the 100 ft by 40 ft converted lighter which was to be her home for the next five years.

Rejuvenation was not readily apparent for the first few months as can be gathered from this account written by your authors the next

summer.

"It is a hot Saturday afternoon, in July 2006 when Rita and I first see Thalatta in dry dock.

She is sitting opposite the boating lake in St. Osyth among a jumble of more modern but less charismatic vessels all vying for the shipyards attention. Stripped of her planking, internal fittings and of course her deck furniture, she looks more like one of the hulks so frequently seen on our shores than the vigorous seagoing barge of a few months before.

Closer inspection shows how heavy wooden frames, looking somewhat like goals at either end of the deck serve as jigs to ensure that everything remains true during the rebuild. All along the sides of the hull the age blackened frames are interspersed with new timbers, bright in their boiled linseed oil finish. Although at the moment alternate frames have been replaced, eventually all will be renewed.

In the evening, conversation with Joe Brannigan, the East Coast Sail Trust Chairman, reveals more details of the state of play and immediate plans. The RSJ forming the keelson has fortunately been found to be sound though this may be extended right the way to the stem post now. The chine's will need to be replaced or repaired, especially where cement had been used to make good some rot in the past! (The chine's, are the timbers forming the angle where the bottom of the barge meets the sides).

It is planned to take out the stem post and replace it as there are so many nails in the existing one that it may not be possible to find anywhere to put the new ones in when the planking is put on! The ceiling (floor of the hold) is also to be replaced.

Peering through the side of the barge from the safety of the boatyard we were surprised to see the cooker from the galley sitting incongruously out of place in the middle of the hold. Many other fittings were piled sadly in a heap at the edge of the boatyard!

All in all, though an interesting afternoon, it felt like visiting a sick friend in intensive care.

When next we pay the old girl a visit it is the middle of August, a little more planking has been removed and some of the interior tidied further. Most noticeable however is the number of new frames which have been added. It now looks as though most of these have been replaced already.

We see more small piles of blackened and rotting wood next to Thalatta, testimony if this were required, to the urgent need for the renovation work to be carried out. Being a Saturday afternoon there is no one at the boatyard to give us permission to go aboard though there is now an entrance to the hull from the pontoon.

We spend a few minutes taking photo's and admiring the shipwrights work before once more leaving the barge in peace."

Not great prose perhaps but hopefully capturing some of the emotion and atmosphere of the occasion.

Chapter Eleven
ECST and the Heritage Lottery Fund

Work of the nature needing to be carried out on *Thalatta* takes money, a lot of money. The project would not have been possible without the Heritage Lottery Fund (HLF) which was set up by Parliament in 1994 to give grants to a wide range of projects involving the local, regional and national heritage of the United Kingdom. HLF distributes a share of the money raised by the National Lottery for Good Causes.

HLF is officially known as a 'non-departmental public body'. This means that, although not a government department, financial and policy directives are issued through the Secretary of State for Culture, Media and Sport and Parliamentary accountability is through his department.

Decisions about individual applications and policies are taken entirely independently of the Government.

HLF is administered by the Trustees of the National Heritage Memorial Fund (NHMF), the fund of last resort for the UK's heritage, coming to the rescue by funding emergency acquisitions. NHMF allocates around £5 million of government grant-in-aid money per year to our national heritage.

From every pound spent on National Lottery tickets, 28p goes directly to good causes for the benefit of communities across the UK. The money is allocated in the following way:

- Charities, health, education the environment: 46%;
- Sports: 18%;
- Arts: 18%;
- Heritage: 18%;

There are currently 13 Lottery funders who independently decide which projects have successfully applied for a grant. Each is independent of Government but has to follow guidelines when deciding who should receive National Lottery funding. (Information from www.hlf.org.uk)

Your authors are indebted to Nick Hayward of ECST for the following account of the role of HLF in *Thalatta's* refurbishment;

"The proposed refurbishment of Thalatta was clearly going to cost more that the ECST could afford and the only way of proceeding was to obtain a large grant. A number of donors were approached – many successfully – but it was clear that main tranche of money would only be available from the National Lottery, specifically the Heritage Lottery Fund.

As guardians of public money HLF will only provide grants to projects which can demonstrate financial viability and community benefit and therefore its acceptance criteria are stringent and demanding. ECST formally applied to HLF in December 2004 and received an offer of a grant of 66% of the total in April 2005 which, following selection of a shipyard on a competitive basis, allowed work to start during the winter of 2005/2006. ECST was required to raise the remaining 33%.

In addition to the detailed application procedure, HLF quite rightly expected to monitor progress regularly, and in our case monthly, to ensure progress matched the plan and spending schedule. It was not long (late 2006), however, before it was discovered that the work required was far more extensive than had previously been estimated because the professional surveyors used when Thalatta was afloat had been unable to investigate the inner recesses of the hull, and much of this was past saving. This dismantling process was exceptionally discouraging but it did reveal clearly how much work was actually needed.

Based on this revelation ECST estimated the additional work as a series of 'Change Requests' to calculate labour and materials costs and the impact on the project plan and sought HLF's agreement to fund an extension to the grant. Having been impressed with the professional nature of the project to that date and seeing clearly the scale of additional work, HLF agreed in March 2007 to increase its grant to a total of £724,000 of the £1,088,000 cost (net of VAT), and work continued on the new plan. It is worth recording that without the HLF funding, ECST would have been compelled to cease operation with Thalatta and her decline into ruin through rot would have been inevitable. A fine vessel – recognised by the National Historic Ships Register – would have been lost to the nation and the community she served for 40 years would have been deprived of the unique experience she provides; she has taken around 10,000 children to sea since retiring from commercial service in the '60's.

August 2011 saw the launch of the refurbished hull after a challenging programme and final, but very detailed, 'fitting-out' work then proceeded through to the Spring of 2012, when Thalatta would become available to resume her work, principally providing cruises for young people.

Chapter Twelve
A Timeline for rebirth

In the following section we will try to give some idea of the timeline for the work carried out. This is based on our own notes taken following visits to the Boatyard with additional material from ECST Newsletters and from an excellent report compiled by Nick Hayward in February 2011.

March 2006

- *Thalatta* moved from Maldon to St.Osyth.
- Gear removed and stored.
- Barge into dry dock.

It was now possible for the first time to truly ascertain the condition

of the oak frames which run the length of the barge. To do this it was necessary to cut through and remove the three layers of planking between each frame. These comprised an inner layer an inch and a half thick which was seriously corroded, a second layer of two inch pitch pine in a sandwich of tarred canvas and an outer layer of planking an inch and a quarter thick. Once the planking had been cut away from between the frames, the remainder which was still attached had to be chiseled away

Sadly it was found that the six inch by eight inch frames had become so corroded that it would be necessary to replace all fifty or so on each side! It was also discovered that the ends of the deck planks had deteriorated more than anticipated and would need to be replaced.

The substantial extra work which was found to be required caused an upward revision of cost estimates to £1,087760. Fortunately HLF agreed to maintain their percentage share so the revised amount needed to be found by ECST was £363,000.

July 06

In pontoon but open to the elements.
- Most of old frames removed and most of the new ones are in place.
- Still some original woodwork around the stern and bow.
- Deck still in place.
- Rotten wood pieces laying around.
- Winches, lee boards etc stored around the yard giving it something of the air of a scrap yard. However the fresh timbers on the barge, standing out brightly against the old wood, do engender a spirit of optimism.

November 06

- By now the badly warn forefoot at the bottom of the stem has been replaced. This is fashioned from Opepe, an African wood widely used in boat building and very resistant to rot.
- The massive Oak stem post has also been replaced.
- A new sternpost and deadwood which fills the gap between it and the underside of the hull have been fitted.
- A polythene tunnel has been purchased and erected to allow winter work to be carried out in relative comfort, protected from the elements.

This polythene tunnel proved to be well "worth it's weight in gold" over the coming years. This greenhouse like structure permitted work to continue almost regardless of the weather all the year round during the main part of the reconstruction work.

Towards the end of the project it was decided to keep *Thalatta* under cover for an extended period to allow painting to be carried out free from the interference of any wet weather this proved to be an exceptionally good decision as it turned out.

Beneficial as this protection was, seeing *Thalatta* eventually released from it was akin to seeing a baby free of an incubator!

Worth its weight in gold the polythene tunnel

February 07

- New frames all in place, including the complex ones forming the shape of the bow.

Straight wood for the frames was easily found but the special shapes required for the curved ones was not.

Eventually the right shaped Oak was found in forests in Suffolk and Norfolk. The saw mill only delivered the straight bits however so Andy had to go up to the forest himself with a chain saw and cut the pieces of timber he needed. Fortunately they were on the ground where the trees had been felled, he did not have to cut them off the tops!

The hardest shapes to find, the right angles, were sourced from a forest near Gosfield, but only after much searching.

- No planking in place yet. The chine keelsons, which run the length of the barge reinforcing the join between her bottom and sides, are now in place. These have been fashioned in Larch, a wood flexible enough to both take the shape of the hull and to flex with it.

July 07

- Work advanced on stern
- Shaped frames in place
- First of new planks being steamed to shape on sides. Although the original planking was of pitch pine, the new planking is of Iroko. Mainly grown in West Africa, this wood is far more readily available nowadays and does the job just as well.
- The method of steaming the planks is one area where modern technology has made life both easier and safer for the shipwright. The curved planking is no longer steamed to shape in a bath and then manhandled into position. Nowadays a polythene bag is used to contain the steam as the timber is shaped as it is fitted in place.
- The Whale, the top plank at the side of the hull is now in place, a key point of reference for the rest of the planking.

Work progressing on the planking

February 08

- First of the curved deck beams in place. These are the timbers that go across the top of the barge to which the deck planking will eventually be fixed. Their curvature gives the deck its camber.
- Lodging knees in place. These are horizontal reinforcements for the deck beams, filling the angle between the beam and the hull side.
- More planking.

Mention has been made of the difficulty in sourcing some of the wood required to fashion the intricate shapes required by a sailing barge a century after their heyday. This difficulty was not confined to wood however, The 9 inch spikes used to secure the planking could only be procured from a firm in Glasgow whilst all the bolts required also had to be specially made to order.

March 09

- Little obvious progress.

This was during a period of 18 months when the basis of further funding from HLF was clarified. To help the smooth flow of this funding ECST changed it's constitution to that of a Company limited by Guarantee. The way in which the charity operated did not change but the Trustees became "Directors" and ECST acquired "Ltd" in it's name.

The Registered Charity number also changed from 263100 to 1128353.

February 2010

With money once more available, work now gathered pace. A visit in February 2010 was rewarded by the sight of encouraging progress.

- *Thalatta* carved on bow.
- Gunwales now in place.
- Deck beams, including the part beams across to the hatch, all in place.
- Some deck planking.
- Work started on the interior of the hold.
- Greenhouse rolled back to expose the forward section.

August 2010

A further visit in the late summer was revealed more noticeable progress still:

- Cover back on.
- Deck planking complete.
- Holes for hatches but no combings (These form the edges to which the hatch is later fitted).

The deck planking is in place with apertures left for hatches.

October 2010

- Last part of the outer whale complete and chain plate positions have been cut in ready for when the galvanised plates return.
- Sikaflex sealant applied throughout including the deck planking.
- Propellers received.
- New engine ordered.
- Discovered that the anchor winch needs to be rebuilt as the centre section of wood is rotten.
- Plans have been prepared for below decks.

March 2011

- Engine and generators installed, but not yet connected.
- Leaders cabins nearly complete.
- Substantial progress on planning and fitting out below deck.

Not least of the tasks required was to draw up the detailed specifications for the electricians, covering all the systems required on board.

June 2011

- Detailed work being carried out on the electronic specifications for equipment below deck. Make and model of the ships freezer agreed, following in depth research.

In depth research included, (but was not confined to) ringing Steve bobbing around in the Pyefleet on *Reminder* and getting him to check on the specs for hers. It says a lot that he was not only prepared to crawl round his galley floor looking for the make and model number, but to do so happily, or at least so it sounded on the phone!

At this time it was decided to keep *Thalatta* in the Dry dock and under the polythene tunnel for longer than previously intended. It was felt that the opportunity should be taken to finish off as much of the exterior painting as possible under cover rather than risking the weather - a very good decision as it turned out.

The painting of *Thalatta* was left in the capable hands of her mate Roger Davies, a professional sign writer when not working on barges. The exceptional standard of finish of the barge's paint and varnish bear tribute to Roger's thorough preparation and attention to detail, not to mention considerable skills.

Roger showed great patience in coping with the needs of various tradesmen and visitors while carrying out his work but woe betide anyone damaging the finished product!

August 2011

On a beautiful sunny morning on the 1 August, *Thalatta* was finally floated out of her dry dock home of the previous five years.

Photos courtesy J Brannigan ECST

Chapter 13
The devil is in the detail!

The launching of a ship or boat is never the end of a story, just of a phase. Although it would be nice to relate that once *Thalatta* had been launched the hard work was over and all that remained was some minor fitting out this was never going to be the case.

Even before the launch of course, a great deal of work had gone into drawing up plans for the below deck area. The project was always a forward looking one, with the objective of equipping *Thalatta* for another hundred years of hard work rather than a restoration to a previous time.

Although the basic layout below deck, the location and numbers of cabins, toilets, the galley etc. was established fairly early on, actually installing the equipment becomes a major task when there are few if any precedents and everything has to be done on a "Design and Build" basis.

For the first time in her career *Thalatta* was to be equipped with central heating and showers! All lighting and interior fittings had to be of a standard and appearance which would make her suitable for corporate entertainment in the winter.

Not only was the gainful employment of the barge during the "Off season" a condition of HLF funding, but it was clear that, in the current economic climate, no charity could afford to operate a vessel only earning revenue for half the year.

An idea of the amount of work required can be gained from a list of just a few tasks undertaken between *Thalatta's* launch and her sea trials:

- Central heating boiler fitted, special exhaust extension fashioned to go through the thick hull of a sailing barge.
- Rudder fitted after replacing the main post and some reshaping to allow for slightly different shape between the stern post and rudder.- *Thalatta* now has two screws instead of one. This gives greater manoeuvrability and allows the use of smaller props giving better bottom clearance.
- New mizzen boom fashioned to replace the rotten original.
- Layout of the galley to be decided including sinks, drainers and positioning of the gas cooker, all ensuring current legislation is complied with.
- Re paint and install lee board winches.
- Test run engine, install and set up hydraulics control box and throttles etc.
- Install echo sounder and new radar.

- Design and construct rope safety rails for the main companionway.
- Dismantle brail winch, shot blast then zinc coat /galvanise.
- New lee boards were constructed to replace the old and tired units. These required the use of the yard crane to hoist them into position.

One of the new lee boards waiting final painting and fitting

This list takes no account of the "routine" work of fitting out rigging, sails, bowsprit, mizzen mast etc, a task made no easier by the subtle changes to *Thalatta's* shape as part of her rebuilding.

One of the by- products of the reconstruction of *Thalatta's* hull was a return to its original shape. Over the years, she had inevitably suffered a degree of "hogging", that is the slight sagging at bow and stern which usually appears in large wooden boats and which can be caused by greater buoyancy in the centre of the barge than at either end.

The new timbers in *Thalatta* are of course not as yet subject to such strains and her now clearly visible sheer gives her previous workmanlike appearance an altogether more elegant look.

The replacement of old waterlogged timbers with new has also had the effect of lightening the hull so there is now a noticeable lessening of *Thalatta's* draft.

These benefits are all very well but when it came to refitting the rigging it did not all fit quite as it had before! Over the years adjustments had of course been made to accommodate the slight changes to shape which had occurred with age. Now that everything was square and as it should be again a few readjustments had to be made!

Fortunately, unusually good weather in February and March 2012 made work above deck both easier and more pleasant than in a normal English spring.(Though inevitably this had to be paid for later in the year - gales for the first school trip!)

Painting below deck proceeded as quickly as was possible given that tradesmen were still hard at work up until *Thalatta's* sea trials. Indeed there were a few finishing touches to be carried out at the time of the first school voyage.

One of the newly fitted crab winches.

Two photographs, the top one taken in 2005, just prior to Thalatta's refit and the lower on her sea trials illustrate subtle changes as her original sheer once more replaces the effects of a century of "hogging". No longer with water-logged timbers she is also drawing noticeably less water.

Below Deck Plans

These illustrations may give some idea of the detail changes made to *Thalatta* to bring her up to date.

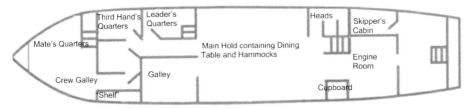

Below deck layout of S.B. Thalatta in 2005

The above diagram shows *Thalatta* as she was in the seasons leading up to her renovation.

The "Shelf" was a spare bunk above the water tank, used if an additional crew member was carried. There was a (very) small additional galley which could be used by the crew while the rather grandly named "Saloon" was used as a merchandising and library area.

The mate had the focs'l whilst as is traditional, the skippers accommodation was at the stern.

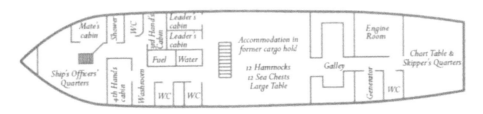

Below deck layout of S.B. Thalatta in 2012

Here we see the below deck plan as drawn up for her renovation. The galley has been moved aft to allow space for an additional leader's cabin and provision for a "Fourth hand's" cabin. Showers have been installed for the first time and the "Heads" are here referred to as W.C.s.

The large wooden dining table and, most importantly of all, the hammocks and sea chests have been retained.

Chapter Fourteen
Good things are worth waiting for!

Some events rush at us as though propelled by an irresistible urge to attain terminal velocity (Dentists appointments and Birthdays spring to mind) Other events seem to take several lifetimes to come about. Tuesday 20 March 2012 very definitely fell into the latter category!

We had known for a few days that skipper Cyril Varley intended to take *Thalatta* out for sea trials today if all was ready. The opportunity to take photographs was not to be missed.

Quite apart from the need to have pictures of the first trip for the ECST, we wanted some for ourselves, and not just for this book!

Having been briefed by Cyril that East Mersea Stone between 1 PM and 3 PM would be a good place and time to take pictures, plans were made and fingers crossed for the weather.

It had been my intention to spend the afternoon on the beach alone waiting for *Thalatta* to make an appearance. Our youngest daughter Kim (aka "The Dart" - so christened by Cyril and Roger due to her shape when she worked on board as a youngster) who lives in Clacton, was also keen to witness the historic event however.

Thus it was that early on this sunny March morning, Kim rang and enquired about the possibility of a picnic on the beach while we waited to take our photos. Eldest daughter Sharron, holidaying at home was also keen so plans were hatched! "I am just going to call in and see Roger and Cyril on my way" says Kim "Lets meet on Mersea Island".

Hurriedly preparations were made, although we had plenty of time before we needed to be at The Stone, there was a little matter of a five metre tide which threatened to come across the Strood (The causeway onto Mersea Island) and cut the mainland off in the late morning.

Sharron and I made our way onto Mersea and headed for the shops. Essential supplies were purchased, provisions for the picknick and most importantly, chocolate! A quick phone call from Kim confirming that she was on her way and a rendezvous at The Glebe was arranged. This done, the three of us proceed to Cudmore Grove Country Park.

Leaving the car, we made our way with picnic gear and of course cameras, down the long grassy slope to the waters edge. With our eyes peeled on the entrance to Brightlingsea Creek in case *Thalatta* sneaked out, we then made our way round the sea wall until we settled on the sandy headland which is Mersea Stone.

Although sunny, the wind was too chilly for us to sit still for too long.

Fortunately Kim had brought along a Frisbee and, food consumed, we kept warm chasing this up and down the beach. At least we did until an over enthusiastic launch took it well out into the river!

Time passed and we began to wonder if *Thalatta* would indeed make an appearance. I was moved to phone Cyril who's response was to ask innocently "Are you at Mersea Stone"? "Yes" "Well look behind you!"

Sure enough, there was *Thalatta*, under almost full sail, sweeping majestically round from West Mersea and past our position, the channel allowing her to come but a few yards from where we stood, cameras clicking furiously.

It is difficult to describe the feeling of delight and satisfaction at seeing the barge in her element once more. For much of her six year refurbishment it had seemed that this day may never come.

There was, by this time, little more than the gentlest of breezes and *Thalatta* was making unhurried progress indeed. We had noticed a small boat following in attendance as the barge approached, this now broke away and nosed into the shore, its prow running up onto the shingle.

A ladder came over the bow together with an invitation to "Climb aboard". This we did with varying degrees of agility but much anticipation.

Our benefactor proved to be young Chris from the boatyard, sent across to pick us up to take more photographs, now with the advantage of being able to position ourselves at will.

Of course now the sun decided that it had shone enough for one day, and the breeze considered that it was time for a rest! Never mind, sometimes the photograph itself is more important than it's technical merit and though full sails and bright sunshine would have been nice we were well satisfied with our work by the time we were returned to the shore.

More importantly than our successful day was the report received that evening from Chris McArthur, the ECST Director tasked with spending the day on board.(Management can be hell sometimes can't it!)

Chris reported that they had motored as far as Osea Island and back before raising sail and that all had gone well. Importantly Cyril and Roger were "Well pleased" with the days work as had been Andy Harman who had also been on board.

The next three pages contain a collection of photographs taken of *Thalatta's* first day of sea trials, we think that they do not need captions.

Chapter Fifteen
Some things never change-thank goodness

So it's a Friday in April 2012 and *Thalatta* is back at Maldon. By some strange co-incidence Rita and I find that it is absolutely essential that we deliver some copies of the latest edition of *"The illustrated guide to Thames sailing barges"* to two of our local customers! It would clearly be wrong not to at least visit the quay side and have a look at the "old girl".

Sure enough, there she is, covered in bunting and as pretty as a picture. Well, OK that is a slight exaggeration as *Thalatta* is parked fourth barge out and we can only see her behind *Wyvenhoe*, *Phoenician* and *Kitty*!

Nevertheless, to see her back at Maldon at all is a great sight and we hope that there is someone on board so that we might be allowed to have a look below decks.

The last time Rita and I were on board was before the great dining table and the rest of the fixtures and fittings had been installed and we are keen to see how she looks now. Sure enough, Roger is spotted and the necessary permission granted. That was of course the easy bit!

Getting to the fourth barge out at Maldon is a bit like competing in some bizarrely sadistic game show. At least it is if you are not in the first flush of youth, unaccustomed to climbing over ropes, cables, masts and chains, or both!

Despite the obstacles we both make it safely on board and find our way below. What greeted us was a sight to make some of us want to wax lyrical about the beauty of natural wood and the carpenters craft, others of us were moved to go and check out the galley!

Not only was the large wooden dining table now in place topped off with a vase of flowers no less, but the children's sea chests, newly painted of course, sat snugly beneath hammocks.

Cyril is off somewhere collecting something we are told, so Roger makes a brew before showing us round. It is not long before the skipper arrives and our help is enlisted in bringing the ships plastic covered foam cushions on board.

Now, just bringing some cushions on board sounds easy, and so it is, if you are next to the quay. As previously related however, making ones way across three barges to get on board is challenging, doing so while carrying a large red seat cushion half as tall as oneself without getting it dirty is in another category altogether.

The true function of lee boards is a mystery to many people. Any one watching on this occasion however would be convinced that their prime function was to act as stepping stones from which to launch oneself from barge to barge whilst hoping to alight in a sufficiently un cluttered area of the next deck to avoid either getting anything dirty or breaking ones neck!

After twenty minutes or so of this jolly entertainment it was time for us to make our way towards other duties and to let the boys get on with the job of preparing *Thalatta* for the coming weeks work.

Somehow it felt that at last things had come full circle and that things were once more returning to the way they should be. Cyril and Roger were preparing to take a party of school children away the following week and, God willing, Rita would be joining them as third hand on two cruises in July. Although there were many times and many reasons when it had not looked possible, the crew that saw the end of one phase of *Thalatta's* service would see the beginning of the next.

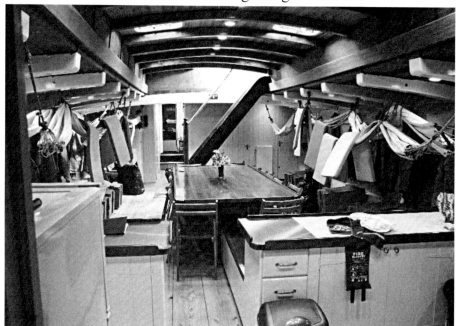

View looking forward from the galley area. Draped over the hammocks are their foam mattresses

Chapter Sixteen
Keith Webb

One of the first tasks for the ECST once *Thalatta* was back in service was to arrange some "Day Sails" so that the many supporters who had helped sustain the project through thick and thin could have the opportunity to enjoy a day savouring the fruits of their endeavours.

One of the first people to book a trip was Mr. E. K "Keith" Webb. Our brief conversation was so interesting that arrangements were made to ring him the following day to provide some material for this book. If the following does not interest the reader as much as it did us the fault is purely in the writing.

Keith (he never uses his first name) was borne into the illustrious barging family of Webb in the year of 1936. Keith's Dad Charlie Webb jnr, Charlie's brothers Ruben and Albie were all barge skippers of note.

In 1951, then fifteen years old, Keith went on board *Thalatta* as cook and third hand. His dad was skipper and Bill Leeks mate.

As cook Keith constantly suffered with sea sickness, something he attributes to the hot and confined conditions in the focs'l where he had to do the cooking- something at least one modern day crew member can identify with!

One of the first dishes the young cook was entrusted with was a delicacy known as "Plum Duff". This was after having been instructed to "Watch how your mother makes it".

It may be helpful here to quote a modern day recipe for the pudding, though it is unlikely the ingredient list was quite so substantial on *Thalatta*!

2 cups self-raising flour
1 teaspoon salt
½ cup brown sugar
½ cup white sugar
2 tablespoons golden syrup
2 teaspoons mixed spice
1½ cups mixed fruit
½ teaspoon baking soda
1 cup chopped vegetable suet
milk, to mix

Directions:

Take a strong cloth and dip in boiling water, then dust cloth thickly with flour and put mixture in cloth and tie securely. Boil for 3 hours.

The result on board when cooked should have been a delicious pudding resembling a football.

Sadly, so sea sick was Keith on this day that one important element of his instruction was forgotten, that of keeping the pot topped up with HOT water to prevent it going off the boil. Several top ups of COLD water later, the pudding was pronounced ready.

No doubt amid much anticipation of the hearty meal to come, the plum duff was unwrapped. Tragedy! Instead of a well rounded and thoroughly cooked football, the muslin cloth yielded a half cooked flat pancake! The cooking lesson was further reinforced with a "Clout round the head" from the skipper who no doubt subscribed to the old saying that

It's not improbable that a man may receive more solid satisfaction from pudding while he is alive than from praise after he is dead.

As with many of the barges, on *Thalatta* the skipper supplied and paid for the food on board deducting a due proportion of the cost from the wages of the crew members. Keith's first wage on *Thalatta* was £2.17s. 0p. whilst as skipper his dad received £5. 10s. 0p. Plus a share in the profits on the cargos carried.

Sometimes it was possible to ease the burden of purchasing essential supplies, as when coal for the ships stove could occasionally be borrowed from one or other of the lighters either at Sheerness or somewhere on the Thames. This was a practice which appears to have been widespread and tacitly accepted by the owners, at least no one ever troubled Keith or his dad!

In many ways the *Thalatta* crew were fortunate in that working for the maltster's, R and W Paul, they were on a weekly wage. Many barge crews were dependent on a share of cargo for payment. In these cases, no cargo meant no work and no pay.

Buoys used by barges waiting for cargos were known as "Starvation buoys" for good reason. The longest Keith was on one of these was six weeks at Woolwich when on *Thistle*.

Most of the trips undertaken by *Thalatta* at this time were between London and Ipswich, usually with a cargo of malt going down to London and wheat, maze or cattle food coming back up to Ipswich.

If there was no work s available from the owners then occasionally their office would arrange a trip working for the London and Rochester Trading Company though this was rare.

There was one notable drama during Keith's early years on board when, probably in 1952, when fighting a strong head wind, far to powerful to raise any sail, the usually faithful 80 hp Ruston diesel engine decided to cease working!

Fortunately for those on board, the ship to shore radio was working and before any serious harm could be done *Thalatta* was towed into the protection of Ramsgate harbour.

The following year Bill Leeks (who only passed away in 2011) moved on and Keith was promoted to mate. This meant extra pay with the added bonus of an end to his sea sickness!

After four years on *Thalatta,* Keith and his Dad moved to the *Jock,* another of Paul's barges.

Built of wood at Ipswich in 1908 by the owners, *Jock* was to have a long and illustrious career. Similar in size to *Thalatta,* she spent most of her life with the Ipswich maltsters though she did have a period with Taylor Woodrow. Her later life in trade was as a motor barge eventually being briefly rigged as a sailing vessel again when she was used for corporate entertainment. After a short time as a floating restaurant, *Jock* was eventually broken up in 2004.

After Charlie Webb left *Thalatta,* a Mr. Haseard took over as skipper to be followed by Bob Wells.

After two years or so on *Jock,* Keith wanted a break from working with his father and enlisted in the army!

Keith volunteered for the role of Air Dispatcher, one of the crew responsible for securing military loads into the wicker panniers parachuted from the rear of the mighty Blackburn Beverly four engine transport planes in use at the time.

With his Barging background it was not surprising that the young soldier showed considerable skill when it came to tying knots. Indeed Keith's skill at securing his loads so impressed his sergeant that it eventually earned him a coveted stripe!

When he left the army at the end of two years Keith returned to life on the barges he loved, serving on Cranfield's *Ethel* and *Marjorie* followed by *Jock* again, then O*live May, Thistle, Phoenician,* and the ex landing craft *Peter Robin* which he described as handling "Like a submarine".

Keith's last two barges were the *Kimberley* and *Orinoco,* both of which he served on as skipper.

Asked which of the barges he preferred Keith said that he-

"Enjoyed all the barges but best were those where the skipper allowed me some responsibility. John Sharman on *Olive May* was good and Dick King of the *Peter Robin* took 5 hours on 5 hours off turns at the helm".

Keith added that he found this latter so enjoyable that he often allowed the skipper to sleep in so he had an extra hour or so at the wheel!

Summing up his experiences on the barges Keith described it as; "The best job I ever did and happy all the while" though he did add the rider that this could depend on the skipper.

When work on the barges started to dry up Keith came ashore to make his fortune as a roofer.

Rita prepares the table for lunch on a pre refurbishment day sail

Several documents relating to *Thalatta's* time in trade survive, and on the next page we have one of the most interesting.

We are grateful to ECST Ltd for supplying this photo copy of part of *Thalatta's* log for the year 1953 when Keith was on board. Entries read:

F R Webb   Master

From	To	Cargo	Sailed	Arrived
Harwich	London	Light	20 Jan 8 am	22 Jan
London	Harwich	670qts barley	24 Jan 7 am	25 Jan
Harwich	London	Light	28 Jan 11 am	29 Jan
London	Harwich	133 tons malt	6 Feb 4.30	8 Feb
Harwich	London	Light	11 Feb8 am	14 Feb
London	Faversham	640qts barley	18 Feb 2 pm	19 Feb
Faversham	London	Light	22 Feb 6.15 am	22 Feb
London	Ipswich	595qts maize	2 March 2.30	6 March
Ipswich	London	Light	8 March 6 am	8 March
London	Ipswich	680qts barley	11 March 2am	12 March
Ipswich	London	Light	18 March 8 am	18 March
London	Ipswich	605qts maize	27 March 2 pm	28 March
Ipswich	London	50 tons malt	5 April 7 am	6 April
London	Ipswich	127 tons maize	20 April 4 pm	24 April
Ipswich	London	Light	8 May 8 am	8 May
London	Ipswich	556qts maize	12 May 1 pm	14 May
Ipswich	London	Light	18 May 6.20 am	19 May
London	Ipswich	711qts barley	4 June 7.30 am	4 June
Ipswich	London	Light	9 June 10.30am	9 June
London	Faversham	135 tons wheat	18 June 7 pm	19 June
Faversham	London	Light	22 June 9 pm	22 June

The regular cargos of wheat, malt, barley and maize clearly reflect the business of her owners R W Paul, the Ipswich maltster's.

In malting, grain is forced to start germinating by being soaked in water. The grain is then dried with hot air to prevent further growth. This process allows the grain's starches to convert to sugars and breaks down proteins into a form which can be used by yeast. Malted grain is used in beers and whiskeys.

Journeys recorded as "light" refer to trips made without a cargo, something clearly to be avoided wherever possible!

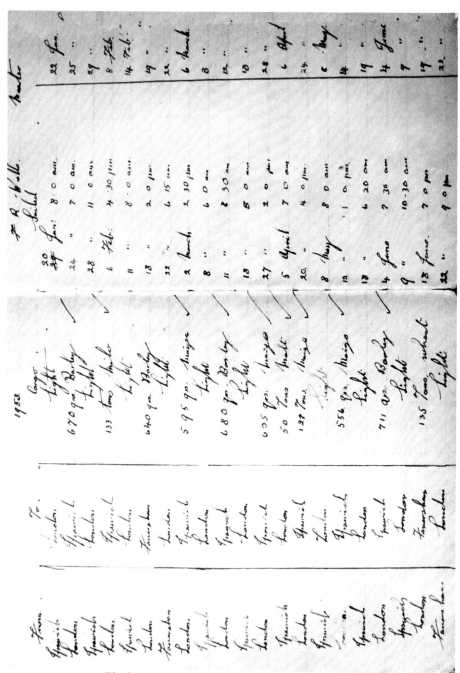

The log entries referred to on the previous page.

Chapter Seventeen
The journey in pictures

So far we have tried to give an idea of the work necessary to carry out *Thalatta's* refurbishment. In this section we would like to take you through a photographic journey from her arrival at St Osyth to her eventual completion and departure on her first Schools Trip.

There were times when it looked like being a very long job indeed! Early days with the old timbers still in the process of being removed.

Even with the new frames in place, it took a certain amount of faith to picture a complete sailing barge.

Traditional skills are kept alive by projects like this. Here naturally curved wood is hand shaped to its final form.

The keelson, the internal backbone of the barge. It also forms an interesting obstacle when moving from one side of the hold to another!

Fitting the planking. The planks wrapped in polythene are being steamed to shape to fit the curves of the hull.

These two views give some idea of the intricate and complex shapes which must be formed at the stern of the barge.

Many of these complex shapes had to be formed from single pieces of timber growing to the right contours wherever possible.

With the planking slowly making its way up the side of the hull, Thalatta starts to look like herself once more.

Slowly but surely the deck beams and their lodging knees are fitted.

*"Open days" provided an opportunity for supporters to see for themselves
how things progressed. Andy Harman explains all!*

*The spikes used to secure Thalatta's planking to her frames.
Not a stock item from B and Q!*

90

Another view of the deck area showing the opening left for the hatch. Visible progress is being made and optimism abounds!

Another tangible sign of progress. At last Thalatta's name is beautifully carved on her bow!

Close up of the transom from the inside showing the skilfully shaped timbers at the stern.

And seen from the outside, showing the colourful decoration traditional on Thames sailing barge transoms.

Brand new diesel engine from Doosan,the South Korean manufacturer specialising in marine diesels

The first stages of fitting out the engine room.

Deck fittings and paintwork begin to sparkle with their new coats of paint or varnish.

Roger Davies is rightly proud of the standard of paintwork sported by Thalatta, seen here as she nears completion.

Roy Swanston from HLF (centre)is shown round by ECST Chairman Joe Brannigan (rear) and Nick Hayward.

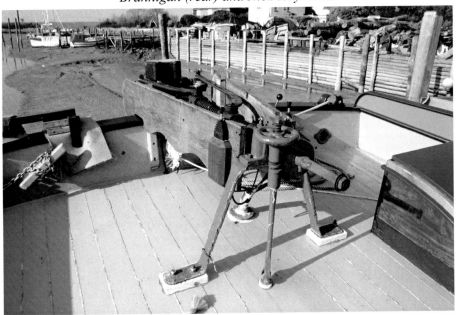

The steering gear nearing completion.

Contrasting views. Looking towards the stern as work progresses before the launch

The same view in the week before Thalatta's first school trip.

What it is all about! Thalatta leaves Maldon on the early morning tide of 16 April 2012 with her first young crew.

Reflection

With the completion of the project came the chance to reflect and for Andy Harman to sum up his feelings looking back on the work.

Asked about the challenges involved in the project Andy confided that he had enjoyed them all though perhaps having to rely on outside tradesmen for things like plumbing and electrics was a little frustrating.

The hardest part of the refurbishment work carried out on *Thalatta* was probably the steaming of the whale strake to the curve necessary to match the bow shape. Formed from 4 inch thick oak, 18 inches wide, the timber had to be steamed in situ for something like four hours as opposed to the one and a half hours needed for the rest of the planking.

Running the whale strake a close second in terms of awkwardness was the fitting of the chine keelsons which form the angle between the sides and bottom of the barge. These timbers which measure 56 feet long, 19 inches wide and 9 inches thick, first had to be threaded through the vertical frames at the bow using a crane and then steamed to the subtle curve of the hull.

Andy considers *Thalatta* to be quite a shapely barge, as is to be expected from a builder who had a reputation for constructing fine smacks among other vessels. One noticeable feature of her hull being what some bargeman would call a "Clipper bow" with a slight curve rather than a dead straight prow. This is obvious from the side view now that she sits high in the water.

There have been more benefits derived from the project than just returning a sailing barge to service. Up to six people worked on *Thalatta* at any one time, not all of whom had started out as shipwrights. Carpenters Dave and Mick had no ship building experience before becoming involved. Both have now acquired considerable extra skills and Mick at least has continued to work on boats.

Two youngsters, Danny and Chris, both under twenty years old learned many new skills working on the project and Danny has stayed in the trade. That Chris has had to has move on to working on the wind farms highlights one of the problems faced at the moment. While it is obviously a good thing to keep traditional skills alive and there will always be some work for the craftsman, unless there is sufficient work to keep them employed full time there is a real risk that the opportunity for their crafts to flourish will be lost.

And Andy? His next project is a canal barge!

Appendix 1 -Landmarks
The following dates have particular significance for Thalatta.

Feb	**1906**	*Thalatta* launched. Builders McLearon of Harwich, owners F Horlock.
Dec	**1908**	Damaged in gale and towed into Lowestoft.
Jan	**1909**	Damaged by steamer *Forth*.
	1914	*Start of World War One*
May	**1917**	Sold to Wynnfield shipping. First engine fitted, now an "auxiliary ketch".
	1918	*End of World War One*
May	**1923**	Purchased by Herbert Body who removed her engine and rigged her as a mulie.
	1926	*John Kemp born*
Aug	**1933**	Sold to R.W. Paul.
	1939	*Start of World War Two*
	1945	*End of World War Two*
	1948	Becomes a "motor barge" when a Ruston and Hornsby diesel fitted, some gear retained.
	1965	*Thalatta's* last full year trading as a cargo carrier.
Oct	**1966**	Last day working as a cargo barge. Purchased by John Kemp and converted for schools use
April	**1967**	First voyage as a schools ship.
	1971	East Coast Sail Trust takes over ownership.
Sept	*1987*	*John Kemp dies*
	1992	*Jane Benham dies*
	2005	Taken out of service by ECST.
	2006	Refurbishment begins at St. Osyth boatyard.
Aug	**2011**	Re launched.
Mar	**2012**	Sea trials commence.
April	**2012**	Returns to service with ECST.

Appendix 2
Surviving barges referred to in the text.

A number of the Thames sailing barges referred to in the text are still with us today:

Alice	Continues to operate as a charter barge from Portsmouth.
Cabby	Charter barge operating from Ipswich and Maldon.
Cambria	Re launched in 2011 after a lengthy restoration.
Cygnet	Based Snape Maltings, only 41 ft long.
Edith May	Another recent restoration, active in Kent.
Edme	Raced by St Osyth boatyard owner, Andy Harman.
Ena	For sale but in poor condition at Hoo in Kent.
Greta	Operates as a charter barge in Kent.
Hydrogen	Very active member of Topsail Charters fleet at Maldon.
Marjorie	Privately owned, Barge Match competitor.
Orinoco	Privately owned, Barge Match competitor.
Phoenician	Privately owned, Barge Match competitor.
Pudge	Owned and operated by The Thames Sailing Barge Trust in Maldon.
Reminder	Very active member of Topsail Charters fleet at Maldon.
Sir Alan Herbert	
	Has now reverted to her original name of *Lady Jean* and is being worked on at Heybridge.
Thistle	Very active member of Topsail Charters fleet at Maldon.
Tollesbury	Privately owned, currently undergoing some restoration.
Wyvenhoe	Privately owned, used for charter and some racing.
Xylonite	Based at Maldon.

For a full account of all the surviving Thames sailing barges please refer to the current edition of *"The illustrated guide to Thames sailing barges"*.

Appendix 3
Thalatta's Skippers

While not necessarily an exhaustive list, the following are referred to in the text .

Skipper	Date	Owner
James Alliston	1906 - 1917	F Horlock
Percy Richmond	1917 - 1918	Wynnfield shipping
Herbert Body	1919 - 1923	Wynnfield shipping
Herbert Body	1923 - 1933	Herbert Body
Fred Grant	Also	Herbert Body
Charles Munn	Also	Herbert Body
Bob Ruffles	1933 - 1946	R W Paul
Joe Lucas	1947 -	R W Paul
Charlie Webb	1951 - 1954	R W Paul
Mr Hastard	1954	R W Paul
Bob Wells	1955 -	R W Paul
Fred Roberts	1966	R W Paul
John Kemp	1967 - 1970	Sailtrust
John Kemp	1971 - 1987	East Coast Sail Trust
Des Kaliszewski		East Coast Sail Trust
Gary Diddams		East Coast Sail Trust
Cyril Varley		East Coast Sail Trust
Kevin Finch		East Coast Sail Trust
Cyril Varley		East Coast Sail Trust

The above are all mentioned in various contemporary or historical texts including, quite heavily John Kemp's *A fair wind for London.* This latter work gives us the names of Fred Grant and Charlie Munn in the period stated but does not give specific dates.

We have tried to piece together dates as best we can but inevitably some are best estimates unless any one can supply further information. John Kemp lists Fred Roberts as being *Thalatta's* "Last professional skipper". We therefore assume that it is his hand that has written the 1965 and 1966 log entries for *Thalatta's* last trips "In Trade".

Appendix 4 - Definitions

Bilge   Space between the bottom of the barge and the ceiling.

Bob   Flag flown from the mast bearing the owners colours.

Brails   Ropes used to furl the mains'l or mizzen. Hence to "Brail up"when reducing sail.

Beam   Width of the barge at its widest point.

Ceiling   Floor of the hold.

Chain plate   Metal plate or strap on the hull to which the rigging is attached.

Chine   Angle between the side and bottom of the barge.

Chine keelson   Beam reinforcing the hull at the chine.

Combings   The wooden edges of the hatches.

Crab   Small winch used for raising and lowering lee boards etc.

Depth   Depth of construction the hull.

Deadwood   Vertical timber at the bottom of the stern.

Draught   Depth of water taken by a vessel.

Floor(s)   Transverse members to which the bottom planking is fastened and which attach to the vertical frames.

Fo'c'sl   Space below deck in the bow which is normally used as the mate's quarters or for storage - or both!

Forefoot   Piece of wood at the base of the stem connecting it with the keelson.

Frames   Vertical timbers which form the framework of the barge.

Gunwale (pron. **Gun'l**)   Top of the sides of the barge.

Horse   Wood or metal beam running across the barge to which the sail is attached but free to travel from side to side.

Hatches   Covers over the hold. Now often fixed making a roof for the below deck area.

Keelson   Lengthwise member running from bow to stern which acts as the backbone of the barge.

Lee boards   Boards carried either side of the hull which are lowered on the down wind (lee) side to give added directional stability by reducing downwind drift.

Lighter   Flat bottomed, un powered vessel for transferring cargo to and from bigger ships.

Lodging knees   Reinforcing pieces between the deck beams and hull.

London river	The Thames.
London mixture	Straw and horse manure cleared from the city's streets and stables.
Maltster	One who makes or sells malt., The partially germinated grain used in brewing etc.
Mizzen	Small sail aft.
Mulie	Barge with sprit rigged mains'l and ketch rigged mizzen.
Reg. Ton (As used here)	Gross registered tonnage. a measure of the internal capacity of a vessel, not to be confused with the weight of cargo which can be carried. Originates from the use of "Tuns" (barrels) of wine as a measure of volume.
Sprit (spreet)	Pole rising at an angle from the base of the mast and supporting the sail.
Stackie	Barge loaded with hay or straw on deck or one designed to be so loaded.
Stem post	Vertical timber in the bow.
Swimmie	Barge with a square bow like a lighter (as with the Colchester based *Fertile*).
Transom	Woodwork across the stern usually colourfully decorated and carrying the barge's name.
Vangs (pron. Wangs)	Wires running from the deck to the sprit top to control its motion.
Whale	Top planks on the side of the barge.
Xylonite	A form of celluloid manufactured by the British Xylonite Co. Hence the name of the barge.

Appendix 5
Other *Thalattas*

In addition to "Our" Thalatta, we have managed to trace some of the many other commercial vessels carrying the same name.

Name	Type	Built	Other information
Thalatta	Fully rigged ship 1771 grt	1881 Built W H Potter in Liverpool	Lost 10/6/1912 off Newfoundland Likely to be the vessel after which the barge is named.
Thalatta	Three mast schooner	1916	Current as "hotel ship" *De Liefde*
Thalatta 1	Three mast schooner with auxiliary motor.	1917	Damaged by U Boat 15/2/1918 Doggerbank (Hit by three shells)
Thalatta	Tanker 3,145 grt	1921	Built as *Empire Tagaya* renamed in 1939, requisitioned by Kreigsmarine 1940. Repatriated 45 returned to original name. Scrapped 1960
Thalatta	Cargo 5671 gt	1922	Oil engine, supply ship WW 2 scrapped 1948
Thalatta	Cargo	1937	Photograph at Friesland 18/8/1996 at www.shipspotting.com
Thalatta	Classic yacht	1949	47' cutter based in Spain.
Thalatta	Cargo 5168 grt	1951 Built Norway	Re named Sol Pemko 1970.
Thalatta	Tanker 18,560 tons	1952	Sold as *Moskeg* in Norway 1954.

A contemporary press report has the "Iron clipper" *Thalatta* leaving Liverpool on 18 April 1890 and arriving in Australia approximately 24 July of that year. A picture in the South Australian state library probably shows this vessel in 1905 listing her as being of 1793 grt.

The "British Barque" *Thalatta* official number 84132 1700 tons reg. Was in collision with the *Record* in 1897 - Board of Trade enquiry records.

The entries for *Thalatta* and *Thalatta 1* look remarkably similar but we have seen no proof that they are the same vessel.

There are various records referring to ships by the name *Thalatta* before this period but we have been unable to find sufficient information to make a worthwhile list.

There are probably many pleasure craft bearing the name *Thalatta* but these have not been researched. Vessels with the name *Thalassa* have also been ignored.